J Rowbotham

A New Guide to German and English Conversation

Modern Phrase, Dialogues, Idioms, Proverbs and a Copious Vocabulary with Tables

of German Moneys, Weights and Measures

J Rowbotham

A New Guide to German and English Conversation
Modern Phrase, Dialogues, Idioms, Proverbs and a Copious Vocabulary with Tables of German Moneys, Weights and Measures

ISBN/EAN: 9783744727518

Printed in Europe, USA, Canada, Australia, Japan

Cover: Foto ©Thomas Meinert / pixelio.de

More available books at **www.hansebooks.com**

A NEW GUIDE

TO

GERMAN AND ENGLISH CONVERSATION;

CONSISTING OF

MODERN PHRASES, DIALOGUES, IDIOMS, PROVERBS,

AND

A COPIOUS VOCABULARY,

WITH

Tables of German Moneys, Weights, and Measures,

FOR THE USE OF

TRAVELLERS, SCHOOLS, AND PRIVATE STUDENTS.

———◆———

By J. ROWBOTHAM, F.R.A.S.

AUTHOR OF A GERMAN GRAMMAR; A FRENCH GRAMMAR; GERMAN LESSONS;
A GUIDE TO SPANISH CONVERSATION; LECTIONES LATINÆ; &C.

———◆———

NEW EDITION, REVISED.

———◆———

LONDON:
DULAU & CO., SOHO SQUARE.

M.DCCC.LXXIII.

PREFACE.

In consequence of the Author's German works having received the flattering approbation of the public, not only in this country, but also in America, where they have been published for the use of Harvard College, he is again emboldened to introduce to its notice the following little work, which he trusts will be found no less useful to the German student than any of his former publications in that language.

As it is generally admitted that the language of conversation differs materially from that which is to be found in books of taste, or on science, it is to be hoped that the following Vocabulary and Dialogues, which are differently arranged from any other extant, will enable the student to acquire more knowledge of the spoken language in a short time, than he possibly could acquire by simply reading standard authors for many years.

The author would not have offered the following pages to the notice of the public, had he not found from experience that the Dialogues in general use are not only deficient of arrangement and classification, but also very defective as far as regards ordinary conversation; the sentences being, for the most part, thrown together as if by accident.

In this work the author has not only endeavoured to classify the subjects of conversation, but he has also attempted to keep up the various Dialogues as naturally as if two persons were occupied in conversing together; and in the Vocabulary the words are so arranged and classified, as almost to supersede the necessity of a dictionary for ordinary purposes, particularly with respect to the names of things in common use.

" With regard to the accuracy of the German part of the present performance, the author has to acknowledge his obligations to several German friends, who not only looked over the work in manuscript, but also revised the sheets while passing through the press."

" The tables of the comparative values of the moneys of the different German States, will, it is hoped, be found useful not only to the merchant and man of business, but also to the traveller, and to students of the German language in general."

Walworth, 1837.

CONTENTS.

	PAGE
The German Alphabet	1
The Articles, Definite, and Indefinite	3
Vocabulary of Nouns	4
Meals. Die Mahlzeiten	ib.
Things used at Tea	ib.
Eatables, etc. at Breakfast	ib.
At Table. Bei Tische	5
Of Eatables at Dinner. Speisen zum Mittagsessen	6
Poultry. Geflügel	7
Game. Wildpret, or Wildbret	ib.
Fish. Fisch	ib.
Vegetables, etc. Gemüse, u. s. w.	8
Spices, etc. Gewürze, u. s. w.	ib.
Of Beverages. Von den Getränken	9
The Dessert. Das Dessert	ib.
Men's Clothing. Von den Männerkleidern	10
Women's Clothes. Von den Frauenkleidern	11
Mankind. Menschengeschlecht	13
Of Kindred, etc. Von Verwandtschaft, u. s. w.	ib.
Of the Human Body, etc. Vom menschlichen Körper, u. s. w.	14
Of the Ppysical Qualities, etc. Von den physischen Eigenschaften, u. s. w.	17
The five Senses. Die fünf Sinne	18
Of the Soul. Von der Seele	ib.
Operations of the Mind. Leidenschaften der Seele	19
Virtues, Vices, etc. Die Tugenden, Laster, u. s. w.	20
The Ages of Man. Das Menschenalter	21
Of God, etc. Von Gott, u. s. w.	ib.
The Universe. Das Weltall	22
The Division of Time, etc. Die Zeiteintheilung, u. s. w.	23
The Seasons. Die Jahreszeiten	24
The days. Die Tage	ib.
The Months. Die Monate	ib.

CONTENTS.

	PAGE
The Elements. Die Elemente	24
Fire, *or* the fire. Das Feuer	25
Air, *or* the air. Die Luft	ib.
Earth, *or* the earth, etc. Die Erde, u. s. w.	ib.
Water, etc. Das Wasser, u. s. w.	26
Of the weather, etc. Von dem Wetter, u. s. w.	27
A city, *or* town. Eine Stadt	28
Of a House. Von einem Hause	29
Furniture of a House. Mobilien eines Hauses	31
Of the Kitchen and Cellar. Von der Küche und dem Keller	32
Precious Stones, *or* Jewels. Die Edelsteine	33
Stones. Die Steine	ib.
Metals. Die Metalle	34
Of Colours. Von den Farben	ib.
Tools, *or* Instruments. Das Handwerkzeug	35
Of Animals. Von den Thieren	36
Of Domestic Animals. Von den häuslichen Thieren	37
Reptiles, Insects, etc. Von den kriechenden Thieren, u. s. w.	38
Of Birds. Von den Vögeln	39
Of Flowers. Von den Blumen	40
Of Trees. Von den Bäumen	41
Of the Country, etc. Vom Lande, u. s. w.	42
Of School. Von der Schule	43
Of Arts, etc. Von den Künsten, u. s. w.	44
The Learned, etc. Die Gelehrten, u. s. w.	ib.
Princes, etc. Fürsten, u. s. w.	45
Titles of Honor. Die Ehrentitel	46
States, etc. Staaten, u. s. w.	47
Of Trades and Professions. Von Gewerben und Handwerken	ib.
Of Commerce. Vom Handel	49
Of Countries and People. Von Ländern und Völkern	51
Of Musical Instruments. Von musikalischen Instrumenten	52
Military Terms. Militair-Benennungen	53
Of Maritime Affairs, etc. Von dem Seewesen, u. s. w.	55
Vocabulary of Adjectives	56
Comparison of Adjectives	58
Vocabulary of Numerals. Cardinal Numbers, etc.	59
Ordinal Numbers	60
Personal Pronouns, etc.	62

CONTENTS. vii

	PAGE
Vocabulary of Verbs	63
Adverbs. Nebenwörter	68
Prepositions. Vorwörter	70
Conjunctions. Bindewörter	71
Interjections. Empfindungswörter	72

SECOND DIVISION.

Seyn, to be conjugated with adjectives, etc.	73
Haben, to have conjugated with nouns	80
Impersonal Verbs	89

THIRD DIVISION.

Familiar Phrases	90
Useful Requests. Nützliche Bitten	ib.
Affirmative Phrases	94
Negative Phrases	97
Interrogative Phrases	99
Imperative Phrases	103
Of Time. Von der Zeit	107
Of Adverbs, etc. Nebenwörter, u. f. w.	108
Examples to illustrate Nouns, etc. of Time	109

FOURTH DIVISION.

Familiar Dialogues	111
Salutations, etc. Die Begrüßungen	ib.
Of Eating and Drinking. Vom Essen und Trinken	114
Breakfast. Das Frühstück	115
Before Dinner. Von dem Mittagsessen	117
Dinner. Das Mittagsessen	119
At Table, or Dinner. Bei Tische	120
The Dessert. Der Nachtisch	130
On Drinking Tea. Beim Theetrinken	133
Supper. Das Abendessen	135
The Evening. Der Abend	137
Of the Weather. Vom Wetter	139
On the German Language. Ueber die deutsche Sprache	142
Of Letter Writing. Vom Briefschreiben	143
With a Woollen Draper. Mit einem Tuchhändler	145
—— Tailor. Mit einem Schneider	147
—— Shoe-maker. Mit einem Schuhmacher	149

CONTENTS.

	PAGE
With a Hatter. Mit einem Hutmacher	151
——— Hosier. Mit einem Strumpfhändler	152
——— Hair-dresser. Mit einem Haarschneider	154
——— Dentist. Mit einem Zahnarzte	ib.
——— Watch-maker. Mit einem Uhrmacher	156
——— Jeweller. Mit einem Juwelier	157
To make Inquiries before undertaking a Journey. Um Erkundigungen einzuziehen, u. s. w.	158
Just on Setting out. Im Begriffe, die Reise anzutreten, u. s. w.	161
The Hours, etc. Die Stunden, u. s. w.	162
To ask the Way. Nach dem Wege fragen	164
On getting up in the Morning. Beim Aufstehen am Morgen	165
Before going to Bed. Ehe man zu Bette geht	167
On Dressing. Beim Ankleiden	168
Between a Lady and her Waiting-maid. Zwischen einer Dame und ihrer Kammerjungfer	169
With a Washer-woman. Mit einer Wäscherin	170
Paying a Visit. Einen Besuch zu machen	173
At Whist. Beim Whistspiel	175
In School. In der Schule	177
To embark in a Packet-boat. Um sich in einem Packetboot einzuschiffen	180
On Embarking, and a Voyage at Sea. Beim Einschiffen und bei einer Seereise	181
Conversation on board a Ship. Gespräch in einem Schiffe	182
Visit of the Custom-house Officers. Visitation, or Besuch der Zollbeamten	183
On hiring, or taking a Lodging. Um eine Wohnung zu miethen	185
Application of Particular Words, such as, An, zu, in, bei, nach, von, u. s. w.	187
So, als, wie, as, like, etc.	188
Als, wie, like, than, how	189
Außer, aber, nur, u. s. w., except, but, etc.	ib.
Proverbs, Idioms, etc.	190
Letters of Invitation, etc. Einladungsbriefe, u. s. w.	193
Explanation of German Coinage	198
Tables of German Moneys	201
——————————Weights	207
——————————Measures	208

A NEW GUIDE

TO

GERMAN CONVERSATION.

THE GERMAN ALPHABET.

Letters.	Names.	Eng. letters.	Pronounced.
U, a	ah	A, a	as *a* in *art;* Ex. Aber, but.
B, b	bäh	B, b	as *b* in English when an initial; but in some provinces as *p* when a final. Ex. Ob, whether, is pronounced *op*.
C c	tsä	C, c	as *k* before a, o, u; but as *ts* before e, i, y. Ex. Cicero, is pronounced *Tsitsero*.
D, d	dä	D, d	as in English when an initial; but like *t* when a final. Ex. Bad, bath, pronounce *Bat*.
E, e	ä	E, e	as *e* in *emblem*. Ex. Erbe, earth.
F, f	eff	F, f	as in English; Ex. Feld, field.
G, g	ghäy	G, g	as in English when an initial; but nearly as *ch* when a final. Ex. Tag, day; is pronounced *tach*.

Observe.—When *a* is marked thus *ä* it is to be pronounced as *a* in *bay;* when not marked at all, it is to be pronounced as *a* in *ah.*

GERMAN ALPHABET.

Letters.	Names.	Eng. letters.	Pronounced.
H, h	hah	H, h	as *h* in *hat*; but in the middle, or at the end of a word it lengthens the sound of the preceding vowel; as Zahn, tooth; sah, saw. After *t* it is mute.
J, i	e or ee	I, i	as *i* in *milk*, or *ee* in *eel*. Ex. Immer, ever, *or* always.
J, j	yod	J, j	as *y* in *young*.
K, k	kah	K, k	as in English, but never mute. Ex. Knabe, boy; Kind, child.
L, l	ell	L, l	as in English. Ex. Leute, people.
M, m	em	M, m	—— „ Mann, man.
N, n	en	N, n	—— „ Name, name.
O, o	o	O, o	—— „ Oben, above.
P, p	pay	P, p	—— „ Platt, flat.
Q, q	koo	Q, q	—— „ Quelle, source.
R, r	err	R, r	—— „ Roth, red.
S, ſ, ß	ess	S, s	—— „ Seife, soap.

N. B. The small ſ, not s, is always used at the end of words; or syllables constituting words.

T, t	tay	T, t	as in English, but *tion* as *ts*. Ex. Nation, nation, is pronounced *natsion*.
U, u	oo	U, u	as *oo* in English. Ex. Zu, to.
V, v	fow	V, v	as *f* —— „ Vater, father.
W, w	vay	W, w	nearly as *v* in *vine*. Ex. Wein, wine.
X, x	eeks *or* iks	X, x	as *x* in *Alexander*.
Y, y	ipsilon	Y, y	as *y* in *syllable*. Ex. Sylbe, syllable.
Z, z	tsett	Z, z	as *ts*. Ex. Zimmer, room, is pronounced *tsimmer*.

The Diphthongs are

German Diphs.			Pronounced.
Ae, ä, *or* ä			as *a* in *hare*. Ex. Bär, *or* Bär, bear.
Oe, ö, „ ö			as *eu* in the French *peu*, little. Ex. Oel, oil, hören, to hear.

ARTICLES.

German Diphs.		Pronounced.
Ue, û, or ü ...		as *u* in the French *du*. Ex. Für, for.
Au, au,	...	as *ou* in *house*. Ex. Haus, house.
Ai, ai, or ay ...		as *y* in *sky*. Ex. Kaiser, emperor.
Ei, ei, „ ey ...		as *y* in *by*. Ex. Freiheit, liberty.
Je, ie,	...	as *ee* in *feet*. Ex. die Biene, the bee.
Eu, eu,	...	as *oi* in *oil*, or *oy* in *boy*. Ex. Leute, people.

THE TRIPHTHONG Aeu, äu, or âu, is sounded like *oi* in *noise*, or *oi* in *oil*. Ex. Häuser, houses: Bäume, trees.

THE DOUBLE OR TRIPLE CONSONANTS.

ch,	sch,	ck,	ff,	ph,	pf,	ss,	sz,	tz.
ch,	sch,	ck,	ff,	ph,	pf,	ss,	sz,	tz.

For further particulars respecting the letters, see the author's German Grammar.

ARTICLES.
INDEFINITE ARTICLES.

	Mas.	Fem.	Neuter.			No plural.
N.	ein,	eine,	ein,	a, *or*	an	——
G.	eines,	einer,	eines, of a, *or* of an			——
D.	einem,	einer,	einem, to a, *or* to an			——
A.	einen,	eine,	ein,	a, *or*	an	——

DEFINITE ARTICLES.

	Mas.	Fem.	Neuter.	Plural.
N.	der,	die,	das,	die, the.
G.	des,	der,	des,	der, of the.
D.	dem,	der,	dem,	den, to the.
A.	den,	die,	das,	die, the.

Observe.—German articles must always agree with the nouns to which they belong, in *gender*, *number*, and *case*. Ex. Ein Vater, *m*. a father; eine Mutter, *f*. a mother; ein Kind, *n*. a child. Der Vater, the father; die Mutter, *f*. the mother; das Kind, *n*. the child.

VOCABULARY OF NOUNS.

Die Mahlzeiten.	MEALS.
Das Frühstück, n.	Breakfast.
Das Mittagsessen, n.	Dinner.
Der Thee, m.	Tea.
Das Abendessen, n.	Supper.

THINGS USED AT TEA.

Eine Tasse, or Theetasse, f.	A cup, or tea-cup
Eine Untertasse, f.	A saucer.
Eine Theekanne, f.	A tea-pot.
Eine Kaffeekanne, f.	A coffee-pot.
Ein Theelöffel, m.	A tea-spoon.
Der Kessel, m.	The kettle.
Die Zuckerschale, f.	The sugar-bason.
Die Zuckerzange, f.	The sugar-tongs.
Eine Eitasse, f.	An egg-cup.

EATABLES, &c. AT BREAKFAST.

Der Thee, m.	Tea.
Der Kaffee, m.	Coffee.
Die Chocolade, f.	Chocolate.
Die Milch, f.	Milk.
Der Rahm, m. die Sahne, f.	Cream.
Das Brod, n.	Bread.
Die Butter, f.	Butter.
Butterbrod, m.	Bread and butter.

Observe.—I. *m.* stands for the *masculine*, *f.* for the *feminine*, and *n.* for the *neuter* gender.

II. Although the most natural arrangement of a Vocabulary would have been to have commenced with the names of things respecting the Universe, yet, in point of utility, the names of things connected with the necessaries of life are of the most importance, especially to those who are desirous of visiting Germany; but who have not sufficient time to acquire an extensive knowledge of the language.

Das geröstete Brod, *n.* — Toast.
Eine Tasse Thee, *n.* — A cup of tea.
Der Zucker, *m.* — Sugar.
Der Hutzucker, *m.* — Loaf-sugar.
Der Honig, *m.* — Honey.
Die Eyer, *or* Eier, *n.* — Eggs.
Der Schinken, *m.* — Ham
Die Zunge, *f.* — Tongue.

Bei Tische.　　AT TABLE.

Das Mittagsessen, *n.* — *Dinner.*

Ein Messer, *n.* — A knife.
Eine Gabel, *f.* — A fork.
Ein Löffel, *m.* — A spoon
Ein Teller, *m.* — A plate.
Eine Schüssel, *f.* — A dish.
Ein Stuhl, *m.* — A chair.
Ein Tischtuch, *n.* — A table-cloth.
Eine Serviette, *f.* — A napkin.
Ein Glas, *n.* — A glass.
Ein Weinglas, *n.* — A wine-glass.
Ein Becher, *m.* — A tumbler.
Ein Salzfaß, *n.* — A salt-cellar.
Eine Caraffine, *f.* Weinflasche, *f.* — A decanter.
Eine Bouteille, *f.* or Flasche, *f.* — A bottle.
Eine Pfefferbüchse, *f.* — A pepper-box.
Ein Senftopf, *m.* — A mustard-pot.
Eine Sauciere, *f.* — A sauce-boat.
Ein Essigfläschchen, *n.* — A vinegar-cruet.
Ein Krug, *m.* — A jug, *or* mug.
Ein Wasserkrug, *m.* — A pitcher.
Ein Korkzieher, *m.* — A corkscrew.

Von den Speisen zum Mittagsessen.

Of Eatables at Dinner.

Das Fleisch, *n.* — Meat.
    Der Braten, *m.* — Roast meat.
    Rinderbraten, *m.* — Roast beef.
    Gekochtes Fleisch. — Boiled meat.
Das Rindfleisch, or Ochsenfleisch. — Beef.
    Beef-steak. — Beef steak.
Das Hammelfleisch, *n.* — Mutton.
    Eine Hammelkeule, *f.* — A leg of mutton.
    Ein Hammelbug, *m.* — A shoulder.
Das Kalbfleisch, *n.* — Veal.
    Kalbs-Coteletts. — Veal-cutlets.
Das Lammfleisch, *n.* — Lamb.
Das Schweinefleisch, *n.* — Pork.
Der Speck, *m.* — Bacon.
    Der Schinken, *m.* — Ham.
    Das Fett, *n.* — The fat.
    Mageres Fleisch, *n.* — Lean meat.
Eine Wurst, *f.* — A sausage.
Die Suppe, *f.* — Soup.
Die Fleischbrühe, *f.* — Broth.
Eine Pastete, *f.* — A pie.
Ein Pudding, *m.* — A pudding.
Eine Blutwurst, *f.* — A black-pudding.
Eine Torte, *f.* Aepfeltorte. — A tart, an apple-tart.
Ein Eierkuchen, *m.* — An omelet.
Das Brod, or Brot, *n.* — Bread.
Der Käse, *m.* — Cheese.
Die Butter, *f.* — Butter.
Eine Schnitte, *f.* — A slice.
Ein Stück, *n.* — A piece.
Ein Bissen, *m.* — A bit, *or* morsel.

OF NOUNS.

Geflügel.	Poultry.
Ein junges Huhn, n.	A chicken, a young fowl.
Ein Flügel, m.	A wing.
Ein Bein, n.	A leg.
Eine Gans, f.	A goose.
Eine Ente, f.	A duck.
Eine Taube, f.	A pigeon.
Ein Truthahn, m.	A turkey.

Wildpret, n.	Game.
Ein Rebhuhn, n.	A partridge.
Ein Fasan, m. or eine Fasane, f.	A pheasant.
Eine Waldschnepfe, f.	A woodcock.
Ein Hase, m.	A hare.
Ein Kaninchen, n.	A rabbit.

Fische, m.	Fish.
Ein Lachs, m.	A salmon.
Eine Makerele, f.	A mackerel.
Ein Kabeljau, m.	A cod-fish.
Eine Steinbütte, f.	A turbot.
Eine Scholle, f.	A sole.
Ein Karpfen, m.	A carp.
Ein Hecht, m.	A pike, or jack.
Eine Forelle, f.	A trout.
Eine Barbe, f.	A barbel.
Ein Aal, m.	An eel.
Eine Auster, f. Austern.	An oyster, pl. oysters.
Ein Hummer, m.	A lobster.
Ein Krebs, m.	A crab.
Eine Garnelle, f.	A shrimp.
Ein Häring, m.	A herring.
Ein Bückling, m.	A red-herring.

Gemüse, n. u. s. w.	Vegetables, &c.
Die Kartoffeln, f. or	Potatoes.
Die Erdäpfel, m.	Potatoes.
Grüner Kohl, n.	Greens.
Der Kohl, m.	Cabbage.
Der Blumenkohl, m.	Cauliflower.
Die Erbsen, f.	Peas.
Die Bohnen, f.	Beans.
Die Schminkbohnen, f.	French-beans.
Der Spinat, m.	Spinach, or spinage.
Der Spargelkohl, m.	Brocoli.
Weiße Rüben, f.	Turnips.
Gelbe Rüben, f,	Carrots.
Der Spargel, m.	Asparagus.
Die Zwiebeln, f.	Onions.
Der Knoblauch, m.	Garlic.
Die Gurken, f.	Cucumbers.
Die Petersilie, f.	Parsley.
Die Rabieschen, m.	Radishes.
Der Lattich, m.	Lettuce.
Der Salat, m.	Salad.
Die Rhabarber, f.	Rhubarb.
Ein Champignon, m.	A mushroom.
Die Gewürze, n. u. s. w.	Spices, &c.
Der Pfeffer, m.	Pepper.
Der Ingwer, m.	Ginger.
Die Gewürznelken, f.	Cloves.
Der Zimmet, m.	Cinnamon.
Die Muskatenblume, f.	Mace.
Der Nelkenpfeffer, m	All-spice.
Muskatennüsse, f.	Nutmegs.
Das Salz, n.	Salt.
Der Senf, m.	Mustard.

OF NOUNS.

Der Essig, *m.* — Vinegar.
Das Oel, *n.* — Oil.
Die Sauce, *f.* — Sauce.
Die Kapern, *f. pl.* — Capers.
Die Anchovis, *f. pl.* — Anchovies.

Von den Getränken. — *Of Beverages.*

Das Wasser, *n.* — Water.
Der Wein, *m.* — Wine.
   Weißer Wein. — White wine.
   Rother Wein. — Red wine.
   Rheinwein. — Hock, *or* Rhenish wine.
   Bordeaux-wein. — Claret.
   Portwein, or Port. — Port wine, *or* Port.
   Xereswein. — Sherry.
   Madeirawein. — Madeira.
   Champagnerwein. — Champagne.
   Burgunderwein. — Burgundy.
   Neuer Wein. — New wine.
   Alter Wein. — Old wine.
Das Bier, *n.* or Bier. — Beer, *or* some beer.
Starkes Bier. — Ale, *or* some ale.
Apfelwein, *m.* — Cider, *or* some cider.
Branntwein, *m.* — Brandy, *or* some brandy.
Der Rum, *m.* or Rum. — Rum, *or* some rum.
Wachholder-branntwein. — Gin, or some gin.
Die Liqueurs, *or* Liqueurs. — Liqueurs.
Das Eis, *n.* or Eis. — Ices, *or* some ices.
Die Limonade, *f.* Limonade. — Lemonade.

Das Dessert, *n.* or der Nachtisch, *m.* — *The Dessert.*

Das Obst, *n.* — Fruit, *or* the fruit.
Ein Apfel, *m.* — An apple.

Eine Birne, f. A pear.
Eine Pflaume, f. A plum.
Eine Aprikose, f. An apricot.
Eine Feige, f. A fig.
Eine Kirsche, f. A cherry.
Eine Traube, f. A grape.
Eine Pfirsche, f. A peach.
Eine Rosine, f. A raisin.
Eine Maulbeere, f. A mulberry.
Eine Erdbeere, f. A strawberry.
Eine Himbeere, f. A raspberry.
Eine Stachelbeere, f. A gooseberry.
Eine Johannisbeere, f. A currant.
Eine Pomeranze, f. Orange. A bitter or Sevilie orange.
Eine Apfelsine, f. An orange.
Eine Mandel, f. An almond.
Eine Wallnuß, f. A walnut.
Eine Nuß, f. A nut.
Eine Kastanie, f. A chestnut.
Eine Oelbeere, f. Olive, f. An olive.
Eine Mispel, f. A medlar.
Eine Melone, f. A melon.
Eine Citrone, f. A lemon.
Eine Zwetsche, f. A prune.

Von den Männerkleidern. *Of Men's Clothing.*

Ein ganzer Anzug, m. A suit of clothes.
Ein Hut, m. A hat.
Ein Halskragen, m. A collar.
Ein Halstuch, n. A cravat.
Eine Halsbinde, . A stock.
Ein Hemd, n. A shirt.
Ein Nachthemd, n. A night-shirt.
Eine Nachtmütze, f. A night-cap.

OF NOUNS.

Ein Schlafrock, *m.*	A dressing-gown.
Ein Rock, *m.*	A coat.
Ein Aermel, *m.*	A sleeve.
Eine Tasche, *f.*	A pocket.
Ein Knopf, *m.*	A button.
Ein Ueberrock, *m.*	A great-coat.
Ein Frack, *m.*	A dress-coat.
Eine Weste, *f.*	A waistcoat.
Die Beinkleider, *n.*	Breeches.
Die Hosen, *f.*	Trousers.
Die langen Beinkleider.	Pantaloons.
Die Unterhosen.	Drawers.
Ein Mantel, *m.*	A cloak.
Die Strümpfe, *m. pl.*	Stockings.
Seidene Strümpfe.	Silk-stockings.
Wollene Strümpfe.	Worsted-stockings.
Ein Strumpfband, *n.*	A garter.
Eine Hemdkrause, *f.*	A frill.
Eine Mütze, *f.*	A cap.
Eine Perrücke, *f.*	A wig.
Ein Taschentuch, *or* Schnupftuch, *n.*	A pocket-handkerchief.
Ein Handschuh, *m.*	A glove.
Ein Schuh, *m.*	A shoe.
Ein Stiefel, *m.*	A boot.
Ein Pantoffel, *m.*	A slipper.
Eine Schnalle, *f.*	A buckle.
Eine Uhr, *f.*	A watch.
Ein Geldbeutel, *m.*	A purse.
Ein Regenschirm, *m.*	An umbrella.
Ein Stock, *m.*	A stick.

    Von den Frauenkleidern.   *Women's Clothes.*

Eine Kleidung, *f.*	A dress.

Ein Kleid, n. — A gown.
Ein Weiberrock, m. — A petticoat.
Ein Unterrock, m. — An under petticoat
Ein Corset, n. — A pair of stays.
Die Schnürbrust, f. — The stays.
   Das Schnürband, n. — The lace.
   Der Stift, m. — The tag.
Ein Halskragen, m. — A tippet.
Ein Schaal, or Shawl, m. — A shawl.
Ein Schleier, m. — A veil.
Ein Muff, m. — A muff.
Ein Kopfputz, m. — A head-dress.
Eine Haube, f. — A cap, or head-dress.
Ein Hut, m. — A bonnet.
   Ein Band, n. — A ribbon.
Eine Schürze, f. — An apron.
Ein Knopf, m. — A button.
Ein Knopfloch, n. — A button-hole.
Die Armbänder, n. — Bracelets.
Ein Ohrring, m. — An ear-ring.
Ein Fächer, m. — A fan.
Ein Ring, m. — A ring.
Ein Juwel, n. — A jewel.
✓ Ein Halsband, n. — A necklace.
   Ein Diamant, n. — A diamond.
Ein Nadelkissen, n. — A pincushion.
✓ Eine Stecknadel, f. — A pin.
Eine Nähnadel, f. — A needle.
Ein Fingerhut, m. — A thimble.
Der Faden, m. — Thread.
Die Baumwolle, f. — Cotton.
Ein Kamm, m. — A comb.
Ein Sonnenschirm, m — A parasol.

OF NOUNS. 13

Das Menschengeschlecht, u. s. w.	*Mankind, &c.*
Ein Mann, m.	A man.
Eine Frau, f.	A woman.
Ein Kind, n.	A child.
Ein kleines Kind.	An infant.
Ein kleines Mädchen, n.	A little girl.
Ein Mädchen, n.	A girl, a maid.
Die Jugend, f.	Youth.
Ein Jüngling, m.	A youth, *or* lad.
Ein junger Mann.	A young man.
Eine junge Frau.	A young woman.
Die Kindheit, f.	Infancy.
Die Mannbarkeit, f.	Puberty.
Das Alter, n.	Old age.
Ein Greis, m.	And old man.
Ein altes Weib, n.	An old woman.
Ein Wittwer, m.	A widower.
Eine Wittwe, f.	A widow.
Ein Riese, m.	A giant.
Ein Zwerg, m.	A dwarf.
Ein Bürger, m.	A citizen.
Ein Meister, m.	A master.
Ein Diener, m.	A man-servant.
Eine Magd, f.	A maid-servant.
Die Geburt, f.	Birth.
Das Leben, n.	Life.
Der Tod, m.	Death.
Von Verwandtschaft, u. s. w.	*Of Kindred &c.*
Der Vater, m.	The father.
Die Mutter, f.	The mother.
Die Aeltern,	The parents.
Der Ehemann, *or* Gemahl, m.	The husband.
Die Gemahlin, *or* Frau, f.	The wife.

Die Ehefrau, or Gattin, f.	The wife.
Der Sohn, m.	The son.
Der Erstgeborne, m.	The eldest son.
Die Tochter, f.	The daughter.
Die Erstgeborne, f.	The eldest daughter.
Der Großvater, m.	The grandfather.
Die Großmutter, f.	The grandmother.
Der Enkel, m.	The grandson.
Die Enkelin, f.	The granddaughter.
Ein Bruder, m.	A brother.
Eine Schwester, f.	A sister.
Ein Oheim, m.	An oncle.
Eine Muhme, or Base, f.	An aunt.
Ein Neffe, m.	A nephew.
Eine Nichte, f.	A niece.
Ein Vetter, m.	A male cousin.
Eine Base, f.	A female cousin.
Eine Familie, f.	A family.
Ein Bräutigam, m.	A bridegroom.
Eine Braut, f.	A bride.
Die Heirath, f.	The marriage.
Die Hochzeit, f.	The wedding.
Ein Verwandte, m.	A relation.
Ein Waise, m. eine Waise, f.	An orphan.
Ein Vormund, m.	A guardian.
Eine Amme, f.	A wet-nurse.

Vom menschlichen Körper und dessen Theilen.	*Of the Human Body and its Parts.*
Ein Glied, n.	A limb *or* member.
Der Kopf, m.	The head.
Das Haar, n.	The hair.
Eine Locke, f.	A lock, *or* curl.
Das Gesicht, n.	The face.

Das Angesicht, n. — The countenance.
Der Schedel m. or Schädel. — The scull.
Das Gehirn, n. — The brain.
Die Stirn, f. — The forehead.
Die Schläfe, f. — The temple.
Das Auge, n. — The eye.
    Der Augapfel, m. — The eyeball, or pupil.
    Das Augenlied, n. — The eyelid.
    Die Augenwimpern, f. — The eyelashes.
    Die Augenbraunen, f. — The eyebrows.
Die Wange, f. or die Backe, f. — The cheek.
Das Ohr, n. die Ohren. — The ear, the ears.
Die Nase, f. — The nose.
    Die Nasenlöcher, n. — The nostrils.
    Die Nasenspitze, f. — The nose end.
Der Backenbart, m. — The whiskers.
Der Mund, m. — The mouth.
    Die Lippen, f. pl. — The lips.
Der Schnurbart, m. — The mustaches.
Der Kinnbacken, m. — The jaw.
    Das Zahnfleisch, n. no pl. — The gum, or gums.
    Ein Zahn, m. — A tooth.
Die Zunge, f. — The tongue.
Der Gaumen, m. — The palate.
Das Kinn, n. — The chin.
Der Bart, m. — The beard.
Der Hals, m. — The neck.
Die Gurgel, or Kehle, f. — The throat.
Der Arm, m. — The arm.
Die Schulter, or Achsel, f. — The shoulder.
    Der Ellbogen, m. — The elbow.
    Das Handgelenk, n. — The wrist.
Die Hand, f. — The hand.
    Die Faust, f. — The fist.

Ein Finger, m.	A finger.
Der Daumen, m.	The thumb.
Der Nagel, m.	The nail.
Der Busen, m.	The bosom.
Die Brust, f. die Brüste.	The breast, the breasts.
Der Magen, m.	The stomach.
Die Nieren, f.	The kidneys.
Die Blase, f.	The bladder.
Die Seite, f.	The side.
Eine Rippe, f.	A rib.
Der Bauch, m.	The belly.
Der Nabel, m.	The navel.
Der Rücken, m.	The back.
Der Rückgrath, m.	The spine.
Der Leib, or Unterleib, m.	The waist.
Die Lende, f. or der Dickschenkel, m.	The thigh.
Das Knie, n.	The knee.
Das Bein, n.	The leg.
Der Fuß, m. die Füße.	The foot, the feet.
Der Enkel, n.	The ankle.
Die Sohle, f.	The sole.
Die Ferse, f.	The heel.
Eine Zehe, f.	A toe.
Die Eingeweide, pl. n.	The entrails.
Das Herz, n.	The heart.
Die Leber, f.	The liver.
Die Lunge, f.	The lungs.
Die Haut, f.	The skin.
Der Leib, m.	The body.
Das Fleisch, n.	The flesh.
Der Knochen, m.	The bone.
Das Mark, n.	The marrow.
Der Muskel, m.	The muscle.
Die Sehnen, f.	The tendrons

Die Nerven, *f.* — The nerves.
Das Blut, *or* Geblüt, *n.* — The blood.
Eine Ader, *f.* — A vein.
Ein Gelenke, *n.* — A joint.

Von ten physischen Eigenschaften, u. s. w. — *Of the Physical Qualities, &c.*

Der Speichel, *m.* — The spittle, *or* saliva.
Die Thränen, *f.* — Tears.
Der Schweiß, *m.* — Sweat, perspiration.
Der Puls, *m.* — The pulse.
Der Hauch, *or* Odem, *or* Athem, *m.* — The breath.
Das Athmen, *n.* — The breathing.
Der Seufzer, *m.* — Sighing, a sigh.
Das Aechzen, *n.* — Groaning, a groan.
Der Schrei, *m.* — A cry, a clamour.
Das Geschrei, *n.* — Crying.
Das Niesen, *n.* — Sneezing.
Der Schlucken, *m.* — The hiccough.
Das Lachen, *or* Gelächter, *n.* — Laughing, laughter, *or* a laugh.
Die Stimme, *f.* — The voice.
Die Sprache, *or* die Rede, *f.* — Speech, *or* the speech.
Der Hunger, *m.* — Hunger.
Der Durst, *m.* — Thirst.
Die Verdauung, *f.* — Digestion.
Der Schlaf, *m.* — Sleep.
Das Schlafen, *n.* — Sleeping.
Das Erwachen, *n.* — Awaking, *or* waking.
Das Schnarchen, *n.* — Snoring.
Ein Traum, *m.* — A dream.
Die Gesichtszüge, *m.* — The features.
Die Gesichtsfarbe, *f.* — The complexion.
Die Gestalt, *f.* der Wuchs, *m.* — The figure, the shape.

Die Geberde, The gesture.
Der Gang, m. The gait.
Die Schönheit, f. Beauty.
Die Häßlichkeit, f. Ugliness.
Die Stärke, or die Kraft, f. Strength or power.
Die Gesundheit f. The health.
Ein frisches Gesicht, n. A ruddy face.
Ein bleiches Gesicht, n. A pale face.

Die fünf Sinne. *The Five Senses.*

Das Gehör, n. Hearing, or the hearing.
Das Sehen, n. Seeing.
Das Gefühl, n. Feeling, or the feeling.
Das Schmecken, n. Tasting, or the taste.
Das Riechen, n. Smelling, or the smell.
Das Gesicht, n. The sight.
Das Fühlen, n. The feeling, or feeling.
Der Geschmack, m. The taste, or tasting.
Der Geruch, m. The smell, or smelling.

Von der Seele. *of the Soul or Mind.*

Die Seele, f. The soul.
Der Verstand, m. The understanding.
Das Gemüth, n. The mind.
Die Einbildung, f. The imagination.
Das Gedächtniß, n. The memory.
Der Wille, m. The will.
Die Vernunft, f. Reason.
Die Urtheilskraft, f. The power of reasoning.
Das Gefühl, n. Sense, feeling.
Das Wissen, n. Knowledge.
Ein Gedanke, m. A thought, an idea.
Das Urtheil, n. The judgment.
Eine Vorstellung f. or ein Begriff, m. An idea.

OF NOUNS. 19

Die Weisheit, *f.*	Wisdom.
Die Wissenschaft, *f.*	Science.
Die Thorheit, *f.*	Folly.
Die Unwissenheit, *f.*	Ignorance.
Die Schwäche, *f.*	Weakness.
Die Dummheit, *f.*	Stupidity.
Leidenschaften der Seele.	*Operations of the Mind.*
Die Liebe, *f.*	Love.
Der Neid, *m.*	Envy.
Der Haß, *m.*	Hatred.
Die Bosheit, *f.*	Malice, wickedness.
Die Rache, *f.*	Revenge.
Der Stolz, *m.*	Pride.
Die Zuneigung, *f.*	Affection.
Die Freundschaft, *f.*	Friendship.
Ein Freund, *m.*	A friend.
Der Glaube, *m.*	Faith.
Die Hoffnung, *f.*	Hope.
Die Barmherzigkeit, *f.*	Charity, mercy.
Die Furcht, *f.*	Fear.
Die Furchtsamkeit, *f.*	Timidity.
Die Verzweiflung, *f.*	Despair.
Die Lustigkeit, *f.*	Mirth, gaiety.
Die Freude, *f.*	Joy, gladness.
Die Ruhe, *f.*	Tranquillity.
Das Vergnügen, *n.*	Pleasure.
Der Kummer, *m.*	Sorrow, grief.
Der Zorn, *m.*	Anger.
Der Zweifel, *m.*	Doubt.
Die Güte, *f.* Gütigkeit, *f.*	Goodness, kindness.
Die Frömmigkeit, *f.*	Piety.
Das Mitleit, *n.*	Compassion.
Der Muth, *m.*	Courage.

Die Tapferkeit, f.	Valour.
Das Gewissen, n.	Conscience.
Die Achtung, f.	Esteem.
Die Wuth, f.	Rage, madness.
Die Gedulb, f.	Patience.
Die Angst, f.	Anxiety.

Die Tugenden, Laster, u.s.w.	*Virtues, Vices, &c.*
Die Wahrheit, f.	Truth.
Die Ehre, f.	Honor.
Der Geiz, m.	Avarice.
Ein Geizhals, m.	A miser.
Die Schuld, f.	Guilt.
Ein Verbrechen, n.	A crime.
Ein Diebstahl, m.	A theft.
Ein Dieb.	A thief.
Die Grausamkeit, f.	Cruelty.
Die Treue, f.	Fidelity, faithfulness.
Die Falschheit, f.	Falsehood.
Die Schelmerei, f.	Knavery.
Die Billigkeit, f.	Equity, justice.
Die Ehrlichkeit, f.	Honesty, probity.
Die Zierlichkeit, f.	Grace, elegance.
Die Heuchelei, f.	Hypocrisy.
Ein Heuchler.	A hypocrite.
Die Gottlosigkeit, f.	Impiety.
Die Unhöflichkeit, f.	Impoliteness, rudeness.
Die Undankbarkeit, f.	Ingratitude.
Die Ungerechtigkeit, f.	Injustice.
Die Unschuld, f.	Innocence.
Die Eifersucht, f.	Jealousy.
Die Bosheit, f.	Wickedness, malice.
Die Verleumdung, f.	Backbiting, slandering.
Das Lügen, n.	Lying.

Eine Lüge. — A lie.
Ein Lügner. — A liar.
Die Bescheidenheit, *f.* — Modesty.
Die Weichlichkeit, *f.* — Effeminacy.
Weichlich. — Effeminate.
Die Faulheit. *f.* — Laziness.
Die Vaterlandsliebe, *f.* — Patriotism.
Ein Vaterlandsfreund, *m.* — A patriot.
Das Vorhersehen, *n.* — Foresight.
Die Einfältigkeit, *f.* — Simplicity.
Die Aufrichtigkeit, *f.* — Sincerity.
Die Mäßigkeit, *f.* — Sobriety.
Die Sorge, *or* Sorgfalt, *f.* — Care.
Die Sorgfältigkeit, *f.* — Carefulness.

Das Menschenalter. — *The Ages of Man.*
Ein Säugling, *m.* — A baby.
Die Kindheit, *f.* — Childhood, infancy.
Die Jugend, *f.* ein Jüngling, *m.* — Youth, a youth.
Das Knabenalter, *n.* — Boyhood.
Die Mannheit, *f.* — Manhood.
Das Alter, *n.* — Old age.
Ein alter Mann, *or* ein Greis — An old man.

Von Gott, u. s. w. — *Of God, &c.*
Gott, *m.* die Götter. — God, gods.
Der Schöpfer, *m.* — The Creator.
Die Vorsehung, *f.* — Providence.
Die Dreieinigkeit, *f.* — The Trinity.
Der Erlöser, *or* Heiland, *m.* — The Saviour.
Jesu Christus, *m.* — Jesus Christ.
Der Heilige Geist, *m.* — The Holy Ghost.
Ein Geist, *m.* — A spirit.
Ein Gespenst, *m.* — A ghost.

Ein Engel, *m.* — An angel.
Der Teufel, *m.* — The devil.
Ein Heiliger, *m.* — A saint.
Ein Prophet, *m* — A prophet
Die Schöpfung, *f.* — The creation.
Der Himmel, *m.* — Heaven.
Die Hölle, *f.* — Hell.
Das Paradies, *n.* — Paradise.
Die Seele, *f.* — The soul.
Der Leib, *m.* — The body.
Die Natur, *f.* — Nature.

Das Weltall. — *The Universe.*

Der Himmel, *m.* — Heaven, *or* the sky.
Das Firmament, *n.* — The firmament.
Ein Planet, *m.* — A planet.
Die Planeten, — The planets.
Die Sterne, *m.* — The stars.
    Ein Stern, *m.* — A star.
Ein Komet, *m.* — A comet.
Die Sonne, *f.* — The sun.
Der Mond, *m.* — The moon.
    Der Neumond *m.* — The new moon.
    Erstes Viertel. — The first quarter.
    Der Vollmond, *m.* — The full moon.
    Letztes Viertel. — The last quarter.
Die Welt, *f.* die Erde, *f.* — The world, the earth.
    Der Nord, *m.* die Mitternacht, *f.* — The north.
    Der Süd, *m.* der Mittag. — The south.
    Der Ost, *m.* der Morgen. — The east.
    Der West, *m.* der Abend. — The west.
Der Lufthimmel, *m. or* Luftkreis. — The atmosphere.
Eine Wolke, *f.* — A cloud.

Die Zeiteintheilung, u. s. w.	*The division* Time, &c.
Ein Jahrhundert, *n.*	An age, *or* a century.
Ein Jahr, *n.*	A year.
Ein Halbjahr.	Half a year.
Ein Vierteljahr.	A quarter of a year.
Ein Monat, *m.*	A month.
Eine Woche, *f.*	A week.
Ein Tag, *m.*	A day.
Eine Stunde, *f.*	An hour.
Eine halbe Stunde.	Half an hour.
Eine Viertelstunde.	A quarter of an hour.
Eine Minute, *f.*	A minute.
Eine Secunde, *f.*	A second.
Ein Augenblick, *m.*	An instant.
Die Morgenröthe, *f.*	The dawn.
Die Dämmerung, *f.*	Twilight.
Der Morgen, *m.*	The morning, the east.
Der Vormittag, *m.*	The forenoon.
Der Mittag, *m.*	Noon, midday, south.
Der Nachmittag, *m.*	The afternoon.
Der Abend, *m.*	The evening, the west.
Die Nacht, *f.*	Night, darkness.
Die Mitternacht, *f.*	Midnight, north.
Sonnenaufgang, *m.*	Sun-rise.
Sonnenuntergang, *m.*	Sun-set.
Tagesanbruch, *m.*	Day-break.
Tageslicht, *n.*	Day-light.
Heute.	To-day.
Gestern.	Yesterday.
Ehegestern, *or* Vorgestern.	The day before yesterday.
Morgen.	To-morrow.
Uebermorgen.	The day after to-morrow.
Der Anfang, *m.*	The beginning.
Das Ende, *n.*	The end.

Die Jahreszeiten.   The Seasons.

Der Frühling, m.	Spring.
Der Sommer, m.	Summer.
Der Herbst, m.	Autumn.
Der Winter, m.	Winter.

Die Tage.   The Days.

Der Sonntag, m.	Sunday.
Der Montag, m.	Monday.
Der Dienstag, m.	Tuesday.
Der Mitwoch, f.	Wednesday.
Der Donnerstag, m.	Thursday.
Der Freitag, m.	Friday.
Der Sonnabend, m. or Der Samstag, m.	Saturday.

Die Monate.   The Months.

Der Januar, m.	January.
Der Februar, m.	February.
Der März, m.	March.
Der April, m.	April.
Der Mai, or May, m.	May.
Der Juni, or Junius, m.	June.
Der Juli, or Julius, m.	July.
Der August, m.	August.
Der September, m.	September.
Der October, m.	October.
Der November, m.	November.
Der December, m.	December.

Die Elemente.   The Elements.

Das Feuer, n.	Fire.

Die Luft, *f.*	Air.
Die Erde, *f.*	Earth.
Das Wasser, *n.*	Water.

Das Feuer.   *Fire.*

Ein Funke, *m.*	A spark.
Die Flamme, *f.*	The flame.
Das Licht, *n.*	Light.
Die Hitze, *f.*	Heat.
Die Kohle, *f.*	Coal.
Der Rauch, *m.*	Smoke.
Der Ruß, *m.*	Soot.
Die Asche, *f. pl.*	Ashes.

Die Luft.   *Air.*

Das Wetter, *n.*	The weather.
Der Wind, *m.*	The wind.
Der Nordwind, *m.*	The north-wind.
Der Südwind, *m.*	The south-wind.
Der Ostwind, *m.*	The east-wind.
Der Westwind, *m.*	The west-wind.
Ein sanfter Wind.	A gentle breeze.
Ein Wirbelwind, *m.*	A whirlwind.
Ein Sturm, *m.*	A storm, *or* tempest.
Eine Windstille, *f.*	A calm.
Ein Orkan, *m.*	A hurricane.
Ein Windstoß, *m.*	A squall.

Die Erde, u. s. w.   *The Earth, &c.*

Der Grund, *m.*	The ground.
Ein Kloß, *m. or* Erdscholle, *f.*	A clod.
Der Staub, *m.*	Dust.
Der Sand, *m.*	Sand.
Der Schutt, *m.*	Rubbish.

Der Kies, m. — Gravel.
Der Thon, m. — Clay.
Der Roth, m, — Mud, mire.
Der Schlamm, m. — Slime, dirt.
Ein Stein, m. — A stone.
   Ein Kieselstein, m. — A pebble, *or* flint.
Ein Felsen, m. — A rock.
Ein Abgrund, m. — A precipice.
Eine Klippe, f. — A cliff.
Ein Thal, n. — A valley, *or* vale.
Eine Ebene, f. — A plain.
Ein Hügel, m. — A hill.
Ein Berg, m. — A mountain.
   Der Gipfel, m. — The summit, *or* top.
   Der Abhang, m. — The declivity.
Eine Schlucht, f. — A hollow, *or* cleft.
Eine Höhle, f. — A cave, *or* cavern.
Ein Cap, m. — A cape.
Ein Vorgebirge, n. — A promontory.
Eine Landenge, f. — An isthmus.
Eine Halbinsel, f. — A peninsula.
Eine Insel, f. — An island.
Die Küste, f. — The coast.
Das Ufer, n. — The bank, *or* shore.
Der Strand, m. *or* das Gestabe, n. — The beach, *or* shore.
Eine Sandbank, f. — A sandbank.

   Das Wasser, u. s. w. — *Water, &c.*

Das Meer, n. die See, f. — The sea.
Der Ocean, m. das Weltmeer, n. — The ocean.
Ein Meerarm, m. — An arm of the sea.
   Die Ebbe und Fluth. — The tide.
   Die Fluth, f. — High-water.

Die Ebbe, *f.* — Low-water.
Die hohen Wellen, *f.* — The surges.
Die Wellen, *or* Wogen, *f.* — The waves, *or* billows.
Der Schaum, *m.* — The foam.
Eine Stille, *f.* — A calm.
Ein Meerbusen, *m.* ein Golf, *m.* — A bay, *or* gulf.
Eine Bay, *f.* — A bay.
Ein Hafen, *m.* — A port, *or* haven.
Eine Meerenge, *f.* — A strait.
Ein Seearm, *m.* — A frith, *or* firth.
Ein Strom, *m.* — A stream, *or* large river.
Ein Fluß, *m.* — A river.
Die Mündung, *f.* — The mouth.
Ein Wildbach, *m.* — A torrent.
Ein Brunnen, *m.* — A fountain, *or* spring.
Ein Bach, *m.* — A rivulet, *or* brook.
Eine Quelle, *f.* — A spring, *or* source.
Ein See, *m.* — A lake.
Ein Teich, *m.* — A pond.
Ein Sumpf, *m.* or Morast, *m.* — A marsh, moor, *or* morass.
Eine Ueberschwemmung, *f.* — A flood, *or* an inundation.
Das See- *or* Meerwasser, *n.* — Sea-water.
Das Regenwasser, *n.* — Rain-water.
Das Quellwasser, *n.* — Spring-water.
Das mineralische Wasser, *n.* — Mineral-water.
Das Salzwasser, *n.* — Salt-water.

Von dem Wetter, u. f. w. — *Of the Weather, &c.*
Die Hitze, *f.* — Heat, *or* the heat.
Die Kälte, *f.* — Cold, *or* the cold.
Die Trockenheit, *f.* — Dryness.
Die Feuchtigkeit, *or* Nässe, *f.* — Humidity, moisture.
Der Dunst, die Dünste, *m.* — The vapour, the vapours.
Der Nebel, Dicke Nebel, *m.* — The mist, fog.

28 VOCABULARY

Der Regen, m.	The rain.
Ein Schauer, m.	A shower.
Ein Gewitter, m.	A storm.
Der Thau, m.	The dew.
Der Frost, m.	The frost.
Ein Reif, m.	A hoar frost.
Das Eis, n.	Ice, or the ice.
Das Thauwetter, n.	Thaw, or the thaw.
Der Schnee, m.	Snow, or the snow.
Der Hagel, m.	Hail, or the hail.
Der Blitz, m.	The lightning.
Der Donner, m.	The thunder.
Ein Donnerschlag, m.	A clap of thunder.
Ein Donnerkeil, m.	A thunderbolt.
Ein Regenbogen, m.	A rain-bow.
Eine Verfinsterung, f.	An eclipse.
Ein Erdbeben, n.	An earthquake.
Ein Feuerspeiender Berg, m.	A volcano.
Das Licht, n.	The light.
Die Finsterniß, or Dunkelheit, f.	Darkness.
Der Schatten, m.	The shade, or shadow.

Eine Stadt, f.   *A City, or Town.*

Ein Kirchspiel, n.	A parish.
Ein Platz, m.	A square, or place.
Eine Straße, f.	A street.
Ein Gäßchen, n.	An alley, or lane.
Eine Universität, f.	A university.
Eine Kirche, f.	A church.
Eine Hauptkirche, f. or ein Dom, m.	A cathedral.
Ein Krankenhaus, n.	A hospital.
Ein Palast, m. or Schloß, n.	A palace.
Das Zollhaus, n.	The custom-house.
Die Bank, f.	The bank.

Die Börse, *f.*	The exchange.
Die Münze, *f.*	The mint.
Die Post, *f. or* Postamt, *n.*	The post-office.
Das Rathhaus, *n.*	The town-hall.
Das Schauspielhaus, *n.*	The theatre.
Ein Theater, *n.*	A theatre.
Ein Schauspiel, *n.*	A play.
Eine Schule, *f.*	A school, *or* academy.
Ein Markt, *m.*	A market.
Ein Gasthaus, *n.*	An inn.
Ein Gasthof, *m.*	An hotel, *or* tavern.
Ein Speisehaus, *n.*	An eating-house.
Ein Kaffeehaus, *n.*	A coffee-house.
Ein Wirthshaus, *n.* eine Schenke, *f.*	A public-house.
Ein Kaufladen, *m.*	A shop.
Ein Bad, *n.*	A bath.
Ein Thor, *n.*	A gate.
Ein Kai, *m. or* Quay.	A quay.
Eine Brücke, *f.*	A bridge.
Die Vorstädte, *f.*	The suburbs.
Ein Kirchhof, *m.*	A church-yard, *or* cemetery.
Ein Grab, *n.*	A grave.
Ein Grabmahl, *n.*	A tomb.
Ein Sarg, *m.*	A coffin.
Eine Grabschrift, *f.*	An epitaph.

    Von einem Hause.   *Of a House.*

Die Freitreppe, *or* Stufen, *f.*	Steps, *or* the steps.
Die Schelle, *or* Klingel, *f.*	The bell.
Der Klopfer, *m.*	The knocker.
Die Thüre, *f.*	The door.
Das Schloß, *n.*	The lock.
Der Schlüssel, *m.*	The key.

Der Riegel, m.	The bolt.
Die Thürangeln, f.	The hinges.
Ein Vorsaal, m.	A hall.
Ein Speisesaal, m.	A dining-room.
Ein Salon, or Saal, m.	A saloon.
Die Treppe, f.	The staircase, or stairs.
Ein Zimmer, n. Gemach, n.	A room, an apartment.
Eine Kammer, f.	A chamber.
Ein Schlafzimmer, m.	A bed-room.
Eine Speisekammer, f.	A pantry.
Die Küche, f.	The kitchen.
Ein Brotschrank, m. or Speiseschrank.	A safe.
Ein Schenktisch, m.	A cupboard.
Der Keller, m.	The cellar.
Eine Dachstube, f.	A garret.
Eine Kinderstube, f.	A nursery.
Ein Laden, m.	A shop.
Die Mauern, f.	The walls.
Ein Fenster, n.	A window.
Der Fußboden, m.	The floor.
Die Pumpe, f.	The pump.
Der Kamin, m.	The chimney.
Das Dach, n.	The roof.
Ein Ziegel, m.	A tile.
Ein Stockwerk, n.	A story, or floor.
Ein Balcon, or Altan, m	A balcony.
Die Bibliothek, f.	The library.
Ein Garten, m.	A garden.
Ein Hof, m.	A yard, or court.
Ein Obstgarten, m.	An orchard.
Ein Brunnen, m.	A well.
Ein Backstein, m.	A brick.
Ein Schiefer, m.	A slate.

OF NOUNS.   31

Mobilien eines Hauses.	*Furniture of a House.*
Ein Tisch, *m.*	A table.
Ein Stuhl, *m.*	A chair.
Ein Armsessel, *m.*	An arm-chair.
Ein Teppich, *m.*	A carpet.
Ein Schirm, *m.*	A screen.
Eine Matte, *f.*	A mat.
Ein Spiegel, *m.*	A looking-glass.
Ein Gemälde, *n.*	A picture.
Eine Schaufel, *f.*	A fire-shovel.
Eine Ofengabel, *f.*	A poker.
Die Feuerzange, *f.*	The tongs.
Der Blasebalg, *m.*	The bellows.
Die Steinkohle, *f.*	Coal, pit coal.
Die Holzkohle, *f.*	Charcoal.
Das Feuer, *n.*	The fire.
Die Flamme, *f.*	The flame.
Der Rauch, *m.*	The smoke.
Die Asche, *f.*	The ashes.
Der Heerd, *m.*	The hearth.
Ein Bett, *n.*	A bed.
Ein Federbett, *n.*	A feather-bed.
Eine Matratze, *f.*	A mattress.
Ein Ohrkissen, Kopfkissen, *n.*	A pillow.
Ein Betttuch, or Bettlaken, *n.*	A sheet.
Die Betttücher, *n.*	The sheets.
Eine wollene Bettdecke, *f.*	A blanket.
Eine Oberdecke, *f.*	A counterpane.
Die Vorhänge, *m. pl.*	The curtains.
Eine Wiege, *f.*	A cradle.
Eine Wärmepfanne, *f.*	A warming-pan.
Ein Leuchter, *m.*	A candlestick.

Ein Licht, n. A candle.
Eine Kerze, f. A wax-candle.
Eine Lampe, f. A lamp.
Eine Kommode, f. A chest of drawers.
Eine Schublade, f. A drawer.
Eine Kiste, f. A box, or chest.
Ein Schrank, m. A cupboard.

Von der Küche und dem Keller. *Of the Kitchen and Cellar.*
Ein Feuerplatz, m. A stove.
Ein Ofen, or Backofen, m. An oven.
Eine Bratpfanne, f. A frying-pan.
Ein Kessel, m. A kettle, or boiler.
Ein Fleischtopf, m. A pot, or pan.
Eine Casserolle, f. A stewpan, or saucepan.
Ein Rost, m. A gridiron.
Ein Dreifuß, m. A trevet.
Ein Bratenwender, m. A jack.
Ein Spieß, m. A spit.
Ein Kochlöffel, m. A ladle.
Ein Reibeisen, n. A grater.
Eine Laterne, f. A lantern.
Der Zunder, m. Tinder, or the tinder.
Eine Zunderbüchse, f. A tinder-box.
Ein Schwefelhölzchen, n. A match.
Ein Feuerstein, m. A flint.
Ein Stahl, m. A steel.
Ein Eimer, m. A pail, or bucket.
Ein Handtuch, n. A towel.
Die Seife, f. The soap, or soap.
Ein Becken, n. A basin.
Ein Wischlappen, m. A dish-cloth.
Ein Wischtuch, n. A duster.
Der Wasserstein, m. The sink.

Eine Tortenpfanne, f.	A baking-dish.
Ein Hackmesser, n.	A cleaver.
Ein Korb, m.	A basket.
Eine Kanne, f.	A pot, *or* can.
Ein Schoppen, m.	A pint.
Ein Faß, n. eine Tonne, f.	A cask.
Ein Fäßchen, n.	A barrel.
Ein Oxhoft n.	A hogshead.
Eine Flasche, *or* Bouteille, f.	A bottle.
Der Pfropfen, *or* Kork, m.	The stopper, *or* cork.

Die Edelsteine, oder Juwelen. — *Precious Stones or Jewels.*

Ein Diamant, m.	A diamond.
Ein Smaragd, m.	An emerald.
Ein Rubin, m.	A ruby.
Ein Amethist, m.	An amethyst.
Ein Saphir, m.	A sapphire.
Ein Türkiß, m.	A turquoise.
Ein Granat, m.	A garnet.
Ein Topaz, m.	A topaz.
Ein Achat, m.	An agate.
Ein Jaspiß, m.	A jasper.
Ein Kristall, m.	A crystal.
Eine Perle, f.	A pearl.

Die Steine, u. f. w. — *Stones, &c.*

Der Marmor, m.	Marble.
Der Gips, m.	Plaster.
Die Kreide, f.	Chalk.
Der Kalk, m.	Lime.
Der Feuerstein, m.	Flint.
Der Schiefer, *or* Schieferstein, m.	Slate.
Der Granit, m.	Granite.

Der Magnet, *m.* — The loadstone.
Die Koralle, *f.* — Coral.
Das Glas, *n.* — Glass.

Die Metalle. — *Metals.*

Das Gold, *n.* — Gold.
Das Silber, *n.* — Silver.
Das Kupfer, *n.* — Copper.
Das Messing, *n.* — Brass.
Das Erz, *n.* — The ore.
Das Eisen, *n.* — Iron.
    Der Rost, *m.* — Rust.
Der Stahl, *m.* — Steel.
Das Bley, *or* Blei, *n.* — Lead.
Die Platina, *f.* — Platina.
Das Blech, *n.* — Tin (*in a pure state*).
Das Eisenblech, *n.* — Tin (*iron tinned over*).
Das Zinn, *n.* — Pewter.
Das Spießglas, *n.* — Antimony.
Der Kobalt, *m.* — Cobalt.
Das Quecksilber, *n.* — Quicksilver.

Von den Farben. — *Of Colors.*

Das Weiß, *n.* Weiß, *adj.* — The white; white.
Das Roth, *n.* Roth, *adj.* — The red; red.
Das Schwarz, *n.* Schwarz, *adj.* — The black; black.
Das Blau, *n.* Blau, *adj.* — The blue; blue.
Himmelblau, *adj.* — Azure, *or* sky-blue.
Das Grün, *n.* Grün, *adj.* — The green; green.
Das Veilchenblau, *n.* Veilchen=Blau, *adj.* — The violet; violet.
Das Gelb, *n.* Gelb, *adj.* — The yellow; yellow.
Der Purpur, *m.* Purpur, *adj.* — The purple; purple.

OF NOUNS.   35

Der Scharlach, *m.* Scharlach, *adj.*   The scarlet, *or* scarlet.
Das Carmesin, *n.* Carmesin, *adj.*   The crimson, *or* crimson.
Das Grau, *n.* Grau, *adj.*   The grey, *or* grey.
Das Braun, *n.* Braun, *adj.*   The brown, *or* brown.

  Das Handwerkszeug.   *Tools, or Implements, &c.*

Ein Hammer, *m.*   A hammer.
Ein Schlägel, *m.*   A mallet.
Eine Säge, *f.*   A saw.
Ein Hobel, *m.*   A plane.
Ein Meißel, *m.*   A chisel.
Ein Bohrer, *m.*   A gimlet.
Ein großer Bohrer.   A wimble, *or* auger.
Eine Axt, *f.*   An axe.
Ein Karst, *m.*   A pick-axe.
Die Zange, *f.*   Pincers.
Ein Amboß, *m.*   An anvil.
Eine Schmiede, *f.*   A forge.
Ein Schraubstock, *m.*   A vice.
Ein Lineal, *n.*   A ruler.
Eine Schuhahle, *f.*   An awl.
Ein Nagel, *m.*   A nail.
Ein Pflug, *m.*   A plough.
Eine Pflugschar, *f.*   A ploughshare.
Ein Pflugeisen, *n.*   A coulter.
Ein Karren, *m.*   A cart.
Ein Wagen, *m.*   A wagon.
  Ein Rad, *n.*   A wheel.
  Eine Achse, *f.*   An axletree.
  Eine Speiche, *f.*   A spoke.
Eine Mauerkelle, *f.*   A trowel.
Ein Zirkel, *m.*   A pair of compasses.
Eine Schraube, *f.*   A screw.
Ein Beil, *n.*   A bill, *or* hatchet.

Ein Dreschflegel, *m.* — A flail.
Ein Grabscheit, *n.* ein Spaten, *m.* — A spade, *or* shov .
Eine Gabel, *f.* — A fork.
Eine Sense, *f.* — A scythe.
Eine Sichel, *f.* — A sickle.
Eine Leiter, *f.* — A ladder.
Eine Angel, *f.* — A fishing-rod.

Von den Thieren. — *Of Animals.*

Ein Thier, *n.* — An animal.
Ein Vieh, *n.* — A beast.
Ein Löwe, *m.* — A lion.
Eine Löwin, *f.* — A lioness.
Ein Elephant, *m.* — An elephant.
Ein Kameel, *n.* — A camel.
Ein Leopard, *m.* — A leopard.
Ein Tiger, *m.* — A tiger.
Ein Wolf, *m.* eine Wölfin, *f.* — A wolf, a she-wolf.
Ein Pantherthier, *m.* — A panther.
Eine Hiäne, *f.* — A hyena.
Ein Rhinoceros, *or* Nasehorn, *n.* — A rhinoceros.
Ein Büffel, *m.* — A buffalo.
Ein Hirsch, *m.* — A stag.
Eine Hirschkuh, *f.* — A hind.
Ein Reh, *n.* — A doe, a deer.
Eine Gemse, *f.* — A chamois.
Ein Biber, *or* Castor, *m.* — A beaver
Eine Fischotter, *f.* — An otter.
Ein Fuchs, *m.* — A fox.
Ein Hase, *m.* — A hare.
Ein Häschen, *n.* — A leveret.
Ein Kaninchen, *n.* — A rabbit.
Ein Affe, *m.* — An ape.
Eine Meerkatze, *f.* — A monkey.

Ein Stachelschwein, *n.*   A porcupine.
Ein Eichhörnchen, *n.*   A squirrel.
Eine Ratte, *f.* or Ratze, *f.*   A rat.
Eine Maus, *f.* Mäuse, *pl.*   A mouse, *pl.* mice.
Ein Maulwurf, *m.*   A mole.
Ein Dachs, *m.*   A badger.

    Von den häuslichen Thieren.   *Of Domestic Animals.*
Ein Pferd, *n.*   A horse.
    Eine Stute, *f.*   A mare.
Ein Klepper, *m.*   A hack-horse.
Ein Maulesel, *m.*   A mule.
Ein Esel, *m.*   An ass, *or* donkey.
Das Vieh, *n.*   Cattle.
Eine Heerde, *f.*   A flock.
Ein Ochs, *m.*   An ox.
Ein Rind, *n.*   A heifer.
Ein Stier, *m.*   A bull.
Eine Kuh, *f.*   A cow.
    Ein Kalb, *n.*   A calf.
Ein Schaf, *or* Schaaf, *n.*   A sheep, a ewe.
Ein Hammel, *m.*   A wether sheep.
    Ein Lamm, *n.*   A lamb.
Eine Ziege, *f.*   A she-goat
Ein Ziegenbock, *m.*   A he-goat.
Ein Ferkel, *n.* Ein Eber, *m.*   A pig, a boar.
Ein Schwein, *n.*   A swine.
Eine Sau, *f.* Mutterschwein, *f.*   A sow.
    Ein Spanferkel, *n.*   A sucking-pig.
Ein Hund, *m.*   A dog.
Eine Hündin, *f.*   A bitch.
    Ein Bullenbeißer, *m.*   A bull-dog.
    Ein Wachtelhund, *m.*   A spaniel.
Ein Hühnerhund, *m.*   A pointer, *or* setter.

Ein Dachshund, m.	A terrier.
Ein Kater, m.	A he-cat, *or* tom-cat.
Eine Katze, f.	A she-cat.
Ein Kätzchen, n.	A kitten.
Das Haar, n.	Hair, *or* the hair.
Die Borsten, f. pl.	The bristles.
Der Fuß, m. pl. die Füße.	The foot, the feet.
Der Schwanz, m.	The tail.
Von den kriechenden Thieren, Insecten, u. s. w.	*Of Reptiles, Insects, &c.*
Eine Schlange, f.	A serpent.
Eine Natter, f.	A snake.
Eine Viper, f.	A viper.
Ein Krokodill, m.	A crocodile.
Eine Eidechse, f.	A lizard.
Ein Frosch, m.	A frog.
Eine Kröte, f.	A toad.
Eine Schnecke, f.	A snail.
Ein Wurm, m.	A worm.
Ein Seidenwurm, m.	A silk-worm.
Eine Raupe, f.	A caterpillar.
Eine Schildkröte, f.	A tortoise.
Ein Blutigel, m.	A leech.
Ein Scorpion, m.	A scorpion.
Eine Spinne, f.	A spider.
Eine Ameise, f.	An ant.
Eine Heuschrecke, f.	A grasshopper.
Eine Biene, f.	A bee.
Ein Schwarm, m.	A swarm.
Ein Bienenkorb, m.	A bee-hive.
Eine Wespe, f.	A wasp.
Eine Mücke, f.	A gnat.
Ein Schmetterling, m.	A butterfly

Eine Motte, f.	A moth.
Ein Floh, m.	A flea.
Eine Wanze, f.	A bug.
Eine Laus, f.	A louse.
Eine Fliege, f.	A fly.
Eine Grille, f.	A cricket.
Ein Käfer m.	A beetle.

Von den Vögeln. — Of Birds.

Ein Vogel, m.	A bird.
Der Schnabel, m.	The bill, or beak.
Der Schwanz, m.	The tail.
Ein Adler, m.	An eagle.
Ein Strauß, m.	An ostrich.
Ein Falke, m.	A falcon.
Ein Geier, m.	A vulture.
Ein Kranich, m.	A crane.
Ein Sperber, m.	A sparrow-hawk.
Ein Rabe, m.	A raven.
Eine Krähe, f.	A crow.
Ein Truthahn, m.	A turkey.
Eine Taube, f.	A dove.
Ein Rebhuhn, m.	A partridge.
Ein Fasan, m.	A pheasant.
Eine Waldschnepfe, Schnepfe, f.	A wood-cock, a snipe.
Eine Gans, f. Gänse, pl.	A goose, Geese, pl.
Eine Ente, f. ein Entrich, m.	A duck, a drake.
Ein Krammetsvogel, m.	A field-fare, or thrush.
Ein Sperling, m.	A sparrow.
Ein Canarienvogel, m.	A canary.
Eine Amsel, f.	A blackbird.
Ein Stahr, m.	A starling.
Eine Nachtigall, f.	A nightingale.
Eine Meise, f.	A tomtit.

Eine Elster, f.	A magpie.
Ein Papagei, m.	A parrot.
Eine Dohle, f.	A jackdaw.
Eine Eule, f.	An owl.
Eine Fledermaus, f.	A bat.
Eine Schwalbe, f.	A swallow.
Eine Feder, f.	A feather.
Ein Nest, n.	A nest.
Ein Käfig, m.	A cage.

Von den Blumen. — Of Flowers.

Eine Blume, f.	A flower.
Ein Blumenstrauß, m.	A nosegay.
Eine Rose, f.	A rose.
Eine Nelke, f.	A pink.
Eine Tulpe, f.	A tulip.
Ein Jasmin, m.	A jessamine.
Ein spanischer Flieder, m.	A lilac.
Eine Hyacinthe, f.	A hyacinth.
Eine Narcisse, f.	A narcissus.
Eine Dreifaltigkeitsblume, f.	A heart's-ease.
Ein Vergißmeinnicht, n.	Forget-me-not.
Eine Ranunkel, f.	A ranunculus.
Eine Himmelsschlüssel, f.	A primrose.
Eine Schlüsselblume, f.	A cowslip.
Eine Sonnenblume, f.	A sun-flower.
Eine Viole, f. ein Veilchen, n.	A violet.
Eine Ringelblume, f.	A marigold.
Eine Lilie, f.	A lily.
Die Maiblume, f.	The lily of the valley.
Die Mirte, f.	The myrtle.
Der Mohn, m.	The poppy.
Der Rittersporn, m.	The lark-spur.
Die Schneeblume, f.	The snow-drop.
Eine Levkoje, f.	A gillyflower, or stock.

Von den Bäumen.   *Of Trees.*

Ein Baum, *m.*	A tree.
Ein Apfelbaum, *m.*	An apple-tree.
Ein Birnbaum, *m.*	A pear-tree.
Ein Pflaumenbaum, *m.*	A plum-tree.
Ein Zwetschenbaum, *m.*	A prune-tree.
Ein Kirschenbaum, *m.*	A cherry-tree.
Ein Aprikosenbaum, *m.*	An apricot-tree.
Ein Nußbaum, *m.*	A nut-tree.
Ein Wall-Nußbaum, *m.*	A walnut-tree.
Ein Pfirsichbaum, *m.*	A peach-tree.
Ein Orangenbaum, *m.*	An orange-tree.
Ein Maulbeerbaum, *m.*	A mulberry-tree.
Ein Eichbaum, *m.* eine Eiche, *f.*	An oak-tree, an oak.
Ein Fichtenbaum, *m.* die Fichte, *f.*	A pine-tree, the pine.
Ein Tannenbaum, *m.* die Tanne, *f.*	A fir-tree, the fir.
Ein Ulmbaum, *m.* eine Ulme, *f.*	An elm-tree, an elm.
Ein Eschenbaum, *m.* die Esche, *f.*	An ash-tree, the ash.
Ein Kastanienbaum, *m.*	A chestnut-tree.
Ein Strauch, *m.*	A shrub.
Ein Stachelbeerstrauch, *m.*	A gooseberry-bush.
Ein Johannisbeerstrauch, *m.*	A currant-tree.
Ein Rosenstrauch, *m.*	A rose-tree.
Ein Weinstock, *m.*	A vine.
Ein Dorn, *m.*	A thorn.
Ein Geißblatt, *n.*	A honeysuckle.
Ein spanischer Flieberbaum, *m.*	A lilac-tree.
Der Lorbeerbaum, *m.*	The laurel.
Der Mirtenbaum, *m.*	The myrtle.
Der Hollunder, *m.*	The elder.
Die Weide, *f.*	The willow.
Die Buche, *f.*	The beech.
Die Pappel, *f.*	The poplar.

Die Linde, f. | The lime.
Die Acacie, f. | The acacia.

Vom Lande, u. s. w. | *Of the Country, &c.*

Ein Dorf. n. | A village.
Ein Weiler, m. | A hamlet.
Eine Wiese, f. | A meadow.
Das Gras, n. | Grass, *or* the grass.
Eine Hecke, f. | A hedge.
Ein Graben, m. | A ditch.
Ein Feld, n. *or* ein Acker, m. | A field.
Ein Gehölz, n. | A wood.
Ein Wald, m. | A forest.
Eine Wüste, f. | A desert.
Ein Obstgarten, m. | An orchard.
Ein Garten, m. | A garden.
Ein Gärtner, m. | A gardener.
Ein Pachtgut, n. | A farm.
Ein Pächter, m. | A farmer.
Ein Schäfer, m. | A shepherd.
Das Korn, n. | Corn.
Der Weizen, m. | Wheat.
Die Gerste, f. | Barley.
Der Hafer, m. | Oats.
Die Bohnen, f. pl. | Beans.
Der Rocken, m. | Rye.
Der Reis, m. | Rice.
Die Erndte, f. | Harvest.
Ein Landmann, m. | A countryman.
Ein Bauer, m. | A peasant.
Ein Arbeiter, m. | A labourer, a workman.
Ein Schloß, n. | A palace, *or* castle.
Ein Landhaus, n. | A country-house.
Eine Strohhütte, f. | A cot, *or* cottage.

Ein Stall, *m.* — A stable.

Von der Schule. — *Of School.*

Ein Buch, *n.*	A book.
Ein Band, *m.*	A volume.
Das Papier, *n.*	Paper.
Ein Bogen Papier.	A sheet of paper.
Ein Buch Papier.	A quire.
Ein Schreibebuch, *n.*	A copy-book.
Eine Blattseite, *f.*	A page.
Die Tinte, or Dinte, *f.*	Ink.
Ein Tintenfaß, *n.*	An inkstand.
Eine Feder, *f.*	A pen.
Der Schnabel, *m.*	The nib.
Eine Stahlfeder, *f.*	A steel-pen.
Ein Federmesser, *n.*	A pen-knife.
Eine Schiefertafel, *f.*	A slate.
Ein Pult, *n.*	A desk.
Eine Lection, *f.*	A lesson.
Eine Aufgabe, *f.*	An exercise.
Ein Brief, *m.*	A letter.
Eine Oblate, *f.*	A wafer.
Das Siegellack, *n.*	Sealing-wax.
Ein Siegel, *n.*	A seal.
Ein Bleistift, *m.*	A black-lead pencil.
Ein Griffel, *m.*	A slate-pencil.
Ein Wort, *n.*	A word.
Eine Silbe, *f.*	A syllable.
Eine Redensart, *f.*	A phrase, an idiom.
Ein Sprichwort, *n.*	A proverb.
Das Komma, *n.*	The comma.
Das Semicolon, or der Strich= punkt.	The semicolon.
Der Doppelpunkt, *m.*	The colon.

Der Punkt, m. — The period.
Eine Übersetzung, f. — A translation.

Von den Künsten, u. s. f. — *Of Arts, &c.*

Eine Wissenschaft, f. — A science.
Eine Kunst, f. — An art.
Die freien Künste. — The liberal arts.
Die mechanischen Künste. — The mechanical arts.
Die Grammatik, f. — Grammar.
Die Weltweisheit, f. — Philosophy.
Die Naturkunde, f. — Physics, natural philosophy.
Die Scheidekunst, or Chemie, f. — Chemistry.
Die Arzneikunst, f. — Medicine.
Die Wundarzneikunst, f. — Surgery.
Die Dichtkunst, f. — Poetry.
Die Geschichte, f. — History.
Die Mathematik, f. — Mathematics.
Die Rechnenkunst, f. — Arithmetic.
Die Buchstabenrechnung, f. — Algebra.
Die Geometrie, or Meßkunst, f. — Geometry.
Die Sternkunde, f. — Astronomy.
Die Baukunst, f. — Architecture.
Die Zeitrechnung, f. — Chronology.
Die Erdbeschreibung, f. — Geography.
Die Redekunst, f. — Rhetoric.
Die Tonkunst, or Musik, f. — Music.
Die Zeichenkunst, or die Zeichnung, f. — Drawing.
Der Tanz, m. das Tanzen, n. — Dancing.
Die Schrift, f. das Schreiben, n. — Writing.

Die Gelehrten, u. s. w. — *The Learned, &c.*

Ein Gelehrter, m. — A learned man.
Ein Philosoph, or Weltweiser, m. — A philosopher.

Ein Steinkundiger, *or* Astronom, *m.*	An astronomer.
Ein Meßkünstler, *or* Geometrist, *m.*	A geometrician.
Ein Sprachlehrer, *or* Grammatiker, *m.*	A grammarian.
Ein Schriftsteller, *m.*	An author.
Ein Geschichtschreiber, *m.*	An historian.
Ein Mathematiker, *m.*	A mathematician.
Ein Dichter, *m.*	A poet.
Ein Kräuterkenner, *m.*	A herbalist.
Ein Botaniker, *m.*	A botanist.
Ein Schulmeister, *m.*	A schoolmaster.
Ein Vernunftlehrer, *or* Logiker, *m.*	A logician.
Ein Lehrer der Redekunst, *m.*	A rhetorician.
Ein Redner, *m.*	An orator.
Ein Baumeister, *m.*	An architect.
Ein Alterthumsforscher, *m.*	An antiquarian.
Ein Scheidekünstler, *or* Chemiker.	A chemist.
Ein Zeichner, *m.*	A draughtsman.
Ein Naturforscher, *m.*	A naturalist.
Ein Lehrer, *or* Professor, *m.*	A teacher.
Ein Prediger, *m.*	A preacher.
Ein Mahler, *m.*	A painter.
Ein Bildhauer, *m.*	A sculptor.
Ein Uebersetzer, *m.*	A translator.
Ein Tonkünstler, *or* Musicus.	A musician.
Ein schöner Geist, *m.* ein Genie.	A man of wit, a genius.
Ein Schauspieler, *m.*	A comedian, *or* player
Ein Dolmetscher, *m.*	An interpreter.

    Fürsten, u. s. f.   *Princes, &c.*

Ein Kaiser, *m.*	An emperor.
Eine Kaiserin, *f.*	An empress.

Ein König, *m.*	A king.
Eine Königin, *f.*	A queen.
Ein Fürst, *m.*	A prince.
Eine Fürstin, *f.*	A princess.
Ein Herzog, *m.*	A duke.
Eine Herzogin, *f.*	A duchess.
Ein Graf, *m.*	A count, *or* an earl.
Eine Gräfin, *f.*	A countess.
Ein Viscount, *or* Vicomte, *m.*	A viscount.
Ein Markis, *m.*	A marquis.
Eine Markisin, *f.*	A marchioness.
Ein Landgraf, *m.*	A landgrave.
Eine Landgräfin, *f.*	A landgravine.
Ein Baron, *or* Freiherr, *m.*	A baron.
Ein Edelmann, *m.*	A nobleman.
Die Edelleute, *m.*	Noblemen.
Ein Ritter, *m.*	A knight.
Ein Gesandter, *m.*	An ambassador.
Ein großer Herr, *m.*	A lord.
Ein Consul, *m.*	A consul.
Ein Advocat, *or* Anwalt, *m.*	A counsellor, barrister.
Ein Richter, *m.*	A judge.
Ein Jurist, *m.*	A lawyer, a jurist.

Die Ehrentitel. *Titles of Honor.*

Mein Herr, *m.* Herr.	Sir, Mr.
Ein Herr.	A gentleman.
Herren.	Gentlemen.
Madame, *f.* Frau, *f.*	Madam, Mrs.
Eine Frau, *f.* eine Dame, *f.*	A lady.
Seine Majestät, *f.*	His Majesty.
Seine Hoheit, *f.*	His Highness.

OF NOUNS. 47

Staaten, u. s. w.   *States, &c.*

Ein Reich, n.   An empire, a kingdom.
Ein Königreich, n.   A kingdom.
Eine Republik, f. or ein freier Staat, m.   A republic, *or* a free state.
Eine Nation, f. Völker, n.   A nation, nations.
Das Volk, n.   The people.
Die französische Völkerschaft.   The French nation.
Eine Colonie, f.   A colony.
Eine Landschaft, f.   A province.
Eine Grafschaft, f.   A county.
Eine Stadt, f.   A city.
Ein Bisthum, n.   A bishopric.

Von Gewerben und Handwerken.   *Of Trades and Professions.*

Ein Gewerbe, n. ein Handel, m.   A trade.
    Ein Händler, m.   A dealer, *or* seller.
    Ein Handelsmann, m.   A tradesman.
    Ein Krämer, m.   A shopkeeper.
Ein Künstler, m.   An artist.
Ein Handwerksmann, m.   A mechanic.
Ein Kaufmann, m.   A merchant.
Ein Cassirer, m.   A cashier.
Ein Unterhändler, *or* Mäkler, m.   A broker.
Staats-Papieren Mäkler, m.   A stock-broker.
Ein Geldmäkler, m.   An exchange-broker.
Ein Schreiber, m.   A clerk.
Ein Bankier, m.   A banker.
Ein Weinhändler, m.   A wine-merchant.
Ein Schlächter, m. *or* Metzger.   A butcher.
Ein Bäcker, m.   A baker.
Eine Gewürzkrämer, m.   A grocer.
Ein Pastetenbäcker, m. Conditor.   A confectioner.

Ein Goldschmid, m.	A goldsmith.
Ein Juwelenhändler, m.	A jeweller.
Ein Buchbinder, m.	A bookbinder.
Ein Buchhändler, m.	A bookseller.
Ein Papierhändler, m.	A stationer.
Ein Buchdrucker, m.	A printer.
Ein Eisenhändler, m.	An ironmonger.
Ein Brauer, m.	A brewer.
Ein Kupferstecher, m.	An engraver.
Ein Uhrmacher, m.	A watchmaker.
Ein Seidenhändler, m.	A mercer.
Ein Hutmacher, m.	A hatter.
Ein Strumpfhändler, m.	A hosier.
Ein Tuchhändler, m.	A woollen-draper.
Ein Schneider, m.	A tailor.
Ein Spezereihändler, m.	A druggist.
Ein Apotheker, m.	An apothecary.
Ein Wundarzt, m.	A surgeon.
Ein Arzt, m. pl. die Aerzte.	A physician, physicians.
Ein Obsthändler, m.	A fruiterer.
Ein Fischhändler, m.	A fishmonger.
Ein Lichtgießer, m.	A tallow-chandler.
Ein Käsekrämer, m.	A cheese-monger.
Ein Müller, m.	A miller.
Ein Papiermacher, m.	A paper-maker.
Ein Zuckersieder, m.	A sugarbaker, or refiner.
Ein Seifensieder, m.	A soap-boiler.
Ein Böttcher, m.	A cooper.
Ein Korbmacher, m.	A basket-maker.
Ein Haarschneider, m.	A hair-dresser.
Ein Barbier, m.	A barber.
Ein Glaser, m.	A glazier.
Ein Lohgärber, m.	A tanner.
Ein Schuster, or Schuhmacher.	A shoemaker.

Ein Schuhflicker, m. — A cobbler.
Ein Messerschmid, m. — A cutler.
Ein Schmid, m. — A smith.
Ein Grobschmid, m. — A blacksmith.
Ein Zimmermann, m. — A carpenter.
Ein Schornsteinfeger, m. — A chimney-sweeper.
Ein Maurer, m. — A mason.
Ein Ladendiener, m. — A shopman.
Ein Lastträger, m. — A porter.
Ein Kutscher, m. — A coachman.
Ein Miethkutscher, m. — A hackney-coachman
Ein Fuhrmann, m. — A wagoner, *or* carman.
Ein Schäfer, m. — A shepherd.
Eine Putzmacherin, f. — A milliner.
Eine Waschfrau, f. — A washerwoman.

Von Handel. — *Of Commerce.*

Die Handlung, f. — Trade, commerce.
Eine Rechnung, f. — An account.
Ein Schuldner, m. — A debtor.
Die Schuld, f. — The debt.
Ein Gläubiger, m. — A creditor.
Der Credit, m. — The credit.
Ein Creditbrief, m — A letter of credit.
Ein Berichtbrief, m. — A letter of advice.
Ein Wechselbrief, m. — A bill of exchange.
Eine Rimesse, f. — A remittance.
Eine Annahme, f. — An acceptance.
Eine Tratte, f. — A draft.
Der Annehmer, m — The accepter.
Der Protest, m. — The protest.
Die Zahlung, f. — The payment.
Ein Rückwechsel, m. — A re-exchange.
Die Bilanz, f. *or* der Saldo, m. — The balance.

Ein Sola=Wechsel, m.	A sola bill of exchange
Eine Handschrift, f.	A promissory note.
Das Geld, m. die Münze, f.	Money, change, coin.
Ein Empfangsschein, m.	A receipt.
Eine Quittung, f.	A quittance, or receipt.
Eine Rechnung, f.	A bill, or an account.
Eine Rechnung salbiren.	To balance an account.
Eine Rechnung bezahlen.	To pay a bill.
Ein Brief, m.	A letter.
Der Tausch, m.	Barter, exchange.
Eine Preisliste, f.	A price-current.
Der Zins, m. or die Zinsen, pl.	Interest, or the interest.
Der Wucher, m.	Usury.
Der Abzug, m.	The discount.
Der Nutzen, or der Gewinn, m.	Profit, gain.
Mäklerlohn.	Brokerage.
Die Assecuranz, f.	The insurance.
Das Assecuranzgeld, n.	The premium.
Eine Factura, f.	An invoice.
Der Kauf, m.	The purchase.
Ein Käufer, m.	A buyer, or purchaser.
Der Verkauf, m.	The sale.
Der Verkäufer, m.	The seller.
Der Preis, m.	The price.
Wohlfeil, Theuer.	Cheap, dear.
Die Billigkeit, f.	The cheapness.
Die Waaren.	Goods, merchandise.
Das Gewicht, n.	Weight.
Ein Handelsgenoß, Associe, m.	A partner.
Eine Handelsgesellschaft, f.	A partnership.
Die Unterzeichnung, f.	The signature.
Ein Bankerot, m.	A bankrupt.
Eine Kunde, f.	A customer.
Der Großhandel, Verkauf im Großen.	Wholesale.

OF NOUNS. 51

Ein Großhändler, m.	A wholesale dealer.
Der Großhandel, m.	The wholesale trade.
Der Verkauf im Kleinen.	Retail.
Ein Kleinhändler, m.	A retailer.

Von Ländern und Völkern. — *Of Countries and People.*

Europa.	Europe.
Ein Europäer.	A European.
Asien.	Asia.
Ein Asier.	An Asiatic.
Afrika.	Africa.
Ein Afrikaner.	An African.
Amerika.	America.
Ein Amerikaner.	An American.
England.	England.
Englisch.	English.
Ein Engländer.	An Englishman.
Eine Engländerin.	An Englishwoman.
Frankreich.	France.
Französisch.	French.
Ein Franzose.	A Frenchman.
Die Franzosen.	The French.
Spanien.	Spain.
Spanisch.	Spanish.
Ein Spanier.	A Spaniard.
Portugal.	Portugal.
Portugiesisch.	Portuguese.
Ein Portugiese.	A Portuguese.
Italien.	Italy.
Italiänisch.	Italian.
Ein Italiäner.	An Italian.
Deutschland.	Germany.
Deutsch.	German.
Ein Deutscher.	A German.

Eine Deutsche.	A German woman.
Holland.	Holland.
Holländisch.	Dutch.
Ein Holländer.	A Dutchman.
Oestereich.	Austria.
Oestereichisch.	Austrian.
Ein Oestereicher.	An Austrian.
Rußland.	Russia.
Russisch.	Russian.
Ein Russe.	A Russian.
Preußen.	Prussia.
Preußisch.	Prussian.
Ein Preuße.	A Prussian.
Pohlen.	Poland.
Ein Pohle.	A Pole.
Eine Pohlin.	A Polish woman.
Die Schweiz.	Switzerland.
Schweizerisch.	Swiss.
Ein Schweizer.	A Swiss.
Schweden.	Sweden.
Schwedisch.	Swedish.
Ein Schwede.	A Swede.
Sachsen.	Saxony.
Sächsisch.	Saxon.
Ein Sachse.	A Saxon.
Von musikalischen Instrumenten.	*Of Musical Instruments.*
Eine Flöte, *f.*	A flute.
Ein Hobois, *n.*	A hautboy.
Eine Clarinette, *f.*	A clarionet.
Eine Pfeife, *f.*	A fife.
Ein Flageolet, *n.*	A flageolet.
Ein Fagott, *n.*	A bassoon.
Eine Trompete, *f.*	A trumpet.

Ein Horn, *n.*	A horn.
Eine Orgel, *f.*	An organ.
Ein Fortepiano, *n.*	A piano, *or* piano-forte.
Eine Harfe, *f.*	A harp.
Ein Clavier, *n.*	A harpsichord.
Eine Guitarre, *f.*	A guitar.
Eine Violine, *f.* eine Geige, *f.*	A violin, a fiddle.
Ein Violoncello, *n.*	A violoncello.
Eine Baßgeige, *f.*	A bass-viol.
Der Bogen, *m.*	The bow.
Eine Trommel, *f.*	A drum.
Eine Pauke, *f.*	A kettle-drum.
Eine Note, *f.*	A note.
Der Ton, *m.* ein Stück, *n.*	The tone, a tune.
Ein Lied, *n.*	A song.
Ein geistliches Lied	A hymn.
Der Gesang, *m.*	The singing.
Ein Concert, *n.*	A concert.
Der Schlüssel, *m.*	The key.

  Militair-Benennungen.   *Military Terms.*

Die Armee, *f.*	The army.
Ein Soldat, *m.*	A soldier.
Der Obergeneral, *m.*	The commander-in-chief.
Ein General, *m.*	A general.
Ein Obrist *m.*	A colonel.
Der Major, *m.*	The major.
Ein Hauptmann, *m.*	A captain.
Ein Lieutenant, *m.*	A lieutenant.
Ein Fähnderich, *m.*	An ensign.
Der Cornet, *m.*	The cornet.
Ein Kriegsbaumeister, *m.*	An engineer.
Ein Unterofficier, *m.*	A subaltern.
Ein Feldwebel *m.*	A serjeant.

Ein Corporal, m.	A corporal.
Der Pfeifer, m.	A fifer.
Ein Trommelschläger, m.	A drummer.
Die Reiterei, f.	The cavalry.
Ein Reiter, m.	A horse soldier.
Das Fußvolk, n.	The infantry.
Ein Regiment, n.	A regiment.
Ein Bataillon, n.	A battalion.
Eine Compagnie, f.	A company.
Die Glieder, n.	The ranks.
Die Reihen, f.	The files.
Eine Schildwache, f.	A sentinel.
Die Artillerie, f.	The artillery.
Ein Lager, n.	A camp.
Ein Zelt, n.	A tent.
Eine Schlacht, f.	A battle.
Ein Krieg, m.	A war.
Ein Bundesgenoß, m.	An ally.
Ein Feind, m.	An enemy.
Die Waffen, f.	Arms.
Eine Kanone, f.	A cannon.
Eine Bombe, f.	A bomb, a shell.
Ein Feuermörser, m.	A mortar.
Eine Flinte, f. ein Gewehr, n.	A gun, *or* musket.
Eine Pistole, f.	A pistol.
Das Pulver, n. *or* Schießpulver.	Powder.
Eine Kugel, f. *or* Flintenkugel.	A ball, *or* bullet.
Eine Lanze, f.	A lance, *or* spear.
Eine Hellebarde, f.	A halberd,
Ein Degen, m.	A sword.
Der Griff, m.	The hilt, *or* handle.
Die Klinge, f.	The blade.
Die Scheide, f.	The sheath.
Ein Bajonet, n.	A bayonet.

Ein Dolch, *m.*	A dagger, *or* poniard.
Ein Feuerstein, *or* Kiesel, *m.*	A flint.
Ein Carabiner, *m.*	A carbine.
Ein Kuraß, *m.*	A cuirass.
Laden.	To charge, *or* load.
Zielen.	To aim.
Losschießen, losbrennen.	To fire *a gun*, &c.

Von dem Seewesen, u. s. w.	*Of Maritime Affairs*, &c.
Die Schiffahrt, *f.*	Navigation.
Ein Schiff, *n.*	A ship.
Ein Fahrzeug, *n.*	A vessel.
Ein Kriegsschiff, *n.*	A man-of-war.
Ein Kauffahrteischiff, *n.*	A merchant-ship, trader, *or* trading-vessel.
Ein Packetboot, *n.*	A packet-boat.
Eine Flotte, *f.*	A fleet.
Die Masten, *m.*	The masts.
Der Hauptmast, *m.*	The mainmast.
Der Anker, *m.*	The anchor.
Der Compaß, *m.*	The compass.
Das Kabel, *n.* or das Kabeltau, *n.*	The cable.
Das Steuerruder, *n.*	The rudder.
Das Segel, die Segel, *n.*	The sail, the sails.
Das Ruder, *n.*	The oar.
Ein Tau, *n.* ein Reif, *m.*	A rope.
Der Helm, *m.*	The helm.
Eine Flagge, *f.*	A flag.
Das Segelwerk, *n.*	The rigging.
Das Verdeck, *n.*	The deck.
Das Vordertheil, *n.*	The prow.
Das Hintertheil, *n.*	The stern.
Das Steuerbord, *n.*	The starboard.
Das Backbord, *n.*	The larboard.

Die Stückpforte, f.   The port-holes.
Ein Admiral, m.   An admiral.
Ein Schiffscapitän, m.   A captain.
Der Botsmann, m.   The boatswain.
Ein Matrose, m.   A sailor.
Ein See-Cadett, m.   A midshipman.
Ein Steuermann, m.   A pilot.
Ein Sturm, m.   A storm.
Ein Ungewitter, m.   A tempest.
Eine Windstille, f.   A calm.
Ein sanfter Wind, m.   A breeze.

VOCABULARY OF ADJECTIVES.

Gut, good.
Schlecht, bad, mean.
Böse, base, bad, wicked.
Gerecht, right, just.
Weise, wise.
Gelehrt, learned.
Fleißig, diligent, industrious.
Geschickt, skilful.
Dumm, stupid, foolish.
Faul, lazy, sluggish.
Müßig, idle.
Unwissend, ignorant.
Süß, sweet.
Bitter, bitter.
Sauer, sour.
Hart, hard.
Weich, soft.
Voll, full.
Leer, empty.

Roth, red.
Schwarz, black.
Gelb, yellow.
Grün, green.
Blau, blue.
Weiß, white.
Grau, grey.
Kurz, short.
Lang, long.
Dünn, thin.
Dick, thick.
Hoch, high, tall.
Groß, great, *or* large.
Klein, small, *or* little.
Stark, strong.
Schwach, weak.
Schön, handsome.
Hübsch, pretty.
Häßlich, ugly.

OF ADJECTIVES. 57

Angenehm, agreeable.
Unangenehm, disagreeable.
Lieblich, lovely.
Liebreich, amiable.
Anmuthig, pleasant.
Glücklich, happy.
Unglücklich, unhappy.
Zufrieden, contented.
Rein, clean.
Schmutzig, dirty.
Feucht, naß, wet.
Trocken, dürre, dry.
Gesund, healthy.
Krank, sick, ill.
Zahm, tame.
Wild, wild.
Fremd, strange.
Heiter, munter, merry.
Traurig, sad, gloomy.
Heilig, holy.
Fromm, pious.
Gerecht, just.
Tugendhaft, virtuous.
Gütig, kind.
Treu, faithful.
Untreu, unfaithful.
Aufrichtig, sincere.
Entheiligend, entweihend, profane.
Falsch, unwahr, false.
Wahr, true.
Stolz, proud.
Weltlich, wordly.
Uebermüthig, vain, haughty.

Dreist, bold.
Sanft, gentle.
Höflich, civil, courteous.
Grob, rude.
Voreilig, rash.
Grausam, cruel.
Barmherzig, merciful.
Mitleidig, compassionate.
Freundlich, friendly.
Gesprächig, leutselig, affable.
Gelehrig, docile.
Dankbar, grateful.
Beständig, constant.
Unbeständig, inconstant.
Nützlich, useful.
Unnütz, useless.
Schuldig, guilty.
Unschuldig, innocent.
Demüthig, humble.
Erhaben, sublime.
Klug, prudent.
Unvorsichtig, imprudent.
Bescheiden, modest.
Züchtig, keusch, chaste.
Blöde, bashful.
Furchtsam, timid.
Tapfer, muthig, courageous.
Verzagt, feige, cowardly.
Betrügerisch, betrüglich, deceitful.
Alt, old.
Jung, young.
Neu, new.
Schwer, heavy, difficult.

Leicht, light, easy.
Warm, warm
Heiß, hot.
Kalt, cold.
Reich, rich.
Arm, poor.
Recht, right.
Link, left.
Müde, weary, tired.

Unordentlich, disorderly.
Toll, mad, senseless.
Unsinnig, insane, frantic.
Sterblich, mortal.
Unsterblich, immortal.
Kindisch, childish.
Sorglos, careless.
Halsstarrig, obstinate.
Sinnreich, ingenious.

COMPARISON OF ADJECTIVES.

The comparative is formed by adding r, or er, to the positive, and the superlative by adding ste, or este; Ex.

Positive.   *Comparative.*   *Superlative.*
Weise, wise; weiser, wiser; der, die, or das weiseste, the wisest.
Klein, little; kleiner, less; der, die, or das kleinste, the least.
Stolz, proud; stolzer, prouder; der, die, or das stolzeste, the proudest.

Observe.—Many adjectives change the vowels a, o, u, into ä, ö, ü, in the comparative and superlative; as,—

Positive.   *Comparative.*   *Superlative.*
Alt, old; älter, older; der, die, or das älteste, the oldest.
Kalt, cold; kälter, colder; der, die, or das kälteste, the coldest.
Roth, red; röther, redder; der, die, or das rötheste, the reddest.
Kurz, short; kürzer, shorter; der, die, or das kürzeste, the shortest.

The following adjectives and adverbs are irregularly formed:—

Positive.   *Comparative.*   *Superlative.*
Gut, good; besser, better; der, die, or das beste, the best.
Hoch, high; höher, higher; der, die, or das höchste, the highest.
Viel, much; mehr, more; der, die, or das mehrste, or meiste, most.
Bald, soon; eher, sooner; der, die, or das eheste, soonest.
Gern, willing; lieber, rather; am liebsten, most willing.

VOCABULARY OF NUMERALS.
Cardinal Numbers.

Ein, *or* eins, one.
Zwei, *or* zwey, two.
Drei, *or* drey, three.
Vier, four.
Fünf, five.
Sechs, six.
Sieben, seven.
Acht, eight.
Neun, nine.
Zehn, ten.

Eilf, *or* elf, eleven.
Zwölf, twelve.
Dreizehn, thirteen.
Vierzehn, fourteen.
Fünfzehn, fifteen.
Sechszehn, sixteen.
Siebzehn, seventeen.
Achtzehn, eighteen.
Neunzehn, nineteen.
Zwanzig, twenty.

Ein und zwanzig. Twenty-one.
Zwei und zwanzig. Twenty-two.
Drei und zwanzig. Twenty-three.
Vier und zwanzig. Twenty-four.
Fünf und zwanzig. Twenty-five.
Sechs und zwanzig. Twenty-six.
Sieben und zwanzig. Twenty-seven.
Acht und zwanzig. Twenty-eight.
Neun und zwanzig. Twenty-nine.
Dreißig. Thirty.
Ein und dreißig. Thirty-one.
Zwei und dreißig. Thirty-two, etc.
Vierzig. Forty.
Ein und vierzig. Forty-one.
Fünfzig. Fifty.
Sechzig. Sixty.
Siebzig. Seventy.
Achtzig. Eighty.
Neunzig. Ninety.
Hundert. A hundred.
Hundert und eins. A hundred and one.

Hundert und zwei. — A hundred and two.
Zwei hundert. — Two hundred.
Zwei hundert und eins. — Two hundred and two.
Drei hundert. — Three hundred, &c.
Tausend. — A thousand.
Zwei tausend. — Two thousand.
Drei tausend und zwei. — Three thousand and two.
Zwanzig tausend. — Twenty thousand.
Hundert tausend. — A hundred thousand.
Eine Million. — A million.
Zwei Millionen, or Million. — Two millions.
Eine Billion. — A billion.
Zwei Billionen, or Billion. — Two billions.

Ordinal Numbers.

The ordinal numbers are formed by adding te to the cardinal, except der erste, *the first;* der dritte, *the third;* but after nineteen ste is added; Ex.

Der, die, or das erste, the first.
Der zweite, the second.
Der dritte, the third.
Der vierte, the fourth.
Der fünfte, the fifth.
Der sechste, the sixth.
Der siebente, the seventh.
Der achte, the eighth.
Der neunte, the ninth.
Der zehnte, the tenth.
Der elfte, eilfte, the eleventh.
Der zwölfte, the twelfth.
Der dreizehnte, the thirteenth.
Der vierzehnte, the fourteenth.
Der fünfzehnte, the fifteenth.
Der sechzehnte, the sixteenth.
Der siebzehnte, the seventeenth.
Der achtzehnte, the eighteenth.
Der neunzehnte, the nineteenth.
Der zwanzigste, the twentieth.
Der ein und zwanzigste, the one and twentieth.
Der zwei und zwanzigste, the two and twentieth.
Der dreißigste, the thirtieth.
Der vierzigste, the fortieth.
Der fünfzigste, the fiftieth.
Der sechzigste, the sixtieth.
Der siebzigste, the seventieth.
Der achtzigste, the eightieth.

OF NUMERALS. 61

Der neunzigſte, the ninetieth.
Der hundertſte, the hundredth.
Der zwei hunderbſte, the two hundredth.
Der tauſenbſte, the thousandth.
Der zwei tauſenbſte, the two thousandth.

Der brei tauſenbſte, the three thousandth. &c.
Der tauſend acht hundert und ſieben und dreißigſte, the one thousand eight hundred and thirty-seventh.

PARTITIVE NUMBERS, &c.

Die Hälfte. — The half.
Das Drittel, or Drittheil. — The third, or the third part.
Das Viertel, or Viertheil. — The fourth, or fourth part.
Ein Fünftel. — A fifth, or $\frac{1}{5}$th.
Ein Zehntel. — A tenth, or $\frac{1}{10}$th.
Drei Viertel. — Three fourths, or $\frac{3}{4}$ths.
Zwei Drittel. — Two thirds, or $\frac{2}{3}$rds.
Ein Paar. — A pair, few, or couple.
Ein Dutzend. — A dozen.
Ein halb Dutzend. — Half a dozen.
Ein Mahl, or einmal. — Once.
Zwei Mahl, or zweimal. — Twice.
Einfach. — Single.
Zweifach. — Double.
Dreifach. — Treble, or threefold.
Anderthalb, for Zweitehalb. — One and a half.
Drittehalb. — Two and a half.
Viertehalb. — Three and a half,
Fünftehalb. — Four and a half, &c.
Erſtlich, erſtens, or zum erſten. — Firstly, or in the first place.
Zweitens, or, zum andern. — Secondly.
Drittens, or zum britten. — Thirdly.
Einzeln. — Singly, or one by one.

Observe.—For further particulars respecting the numerals, see the author's German Grammar.

VOCABULARY OF PRONOUNS.
Personal Pronouns.

FIRST PERSON.

Singular.
N. Jch, I.
G. Meiner, of me.
D. Mir, to me.
A. Mich, me.

Plural.
N. Wir, we.
G. Unser, of us.
D. Uns, to us.
A. Uns, us.

SECOND PERSON.

Singular.
N. Du, thou.
G. Deiner, of thee.
D. Dir, to thee.
A. Dich, thee.

Plural.
N. Jhr, you.
G. Euer, of you.
D. Euch, to you.
A. Euch, you.

THIRD PERSON.

Singular.

	Mas.	Fem.	Neuter.
N.	Er, he.	Sie, she	Es, it.
G.	Seiner, of him.	ihrer, of her.	seiner, of it.
D.	Jhm, to him.	ihr, to her.	ihm, to it.
A.	Jhn, him	sie, she.	es, it.

Plural.

Mas. Fem. & Neut.
N. Sie, they or you.
G. Jhrer, of them.
D. Jnen, to them.
A. Sie, them or you

Observe.—Er, sie, ihn, are sometimes translated by *it*.

Conjunctive Possessive Pronouns.

	Singular.		*Plural.*
Mas	Fem.	Neut.	Mas. Fem. & Neut.
Mein,	meine,	mein,	meine, my.
Dein,	deine,	dein,	deine thy.
Sein,	seine,	sein,	seine, his, its.
Jhr,	ihre,	ihr,	ihre, her.
Unser,	unsere, unsre,	unser,	unsre, our.
Euer,	euere, eure,	euer,	euere, your.
Jhr,	ihre,	ihr,	ihre, their.

Relative Possessive Pronouns.

	Singular.		Plural.
Mas.	Fem.	Neuter.	Mas. Fem. & Neut.
Der meinige,	die meinige,	das meinige,	die meinigen, mine.
Der deinige,	die deinige,	das deinige,	die deinigen, thine.
Der seinige,	die seinige,	das seinige,	die seinigen, his, its.
Der ihrige,	die ihrige,	das ihrige,	die ihrigen, hers, its.
Der unsrige,	die unsrige,	das unsrige,	die unsrigen, ours.
Der eurige,	die eurige,	das eurige,	die eurigen, yours.
Der ihrige,	die ihrige,	das ihrige,	die ihrigen, theirs.

Demonstrative Pronouns.

	Singular.			Plural.	
Mas.	Fem.	Neut.	Mas.	Fem.	Neut.
Der,	die,	das,	die, who, which, that, those.		
Welcher,	welche,	welches,	welche, who, which, that, &c.		
Jener,	jene,	jenes, that.	jene, those.		

Wer, who, whoever, he who, which. *Neut*, Was, that, what, which.

Wer? who? Was? what? Welcher? which? Was für ein? what?

Man, one, some one, we, people, man, they, &c.

Jemand, somebody; Niemand, nobody; Jedermann, every body.

VOCABULARY OF VERBS.

Regular Verbs in General Use.

Achten.	To respect, *or* esteem.
Antworten.	To answer.
Arbeiten.	To labor, *or* work.
Bauen.	To build.
Bedauern.	To pity, to have pity.

Bestrafen.	To punish.
Bessern.	To improve.
Betteln.	to beg *alms*.
Bluten.	To bleed.
Borgen.	To borrow.
Buchstabieren.	To spell.
Darben.	To be in want, to starve.
Dienen.	To serve.
Doppeln.	To double.
Drohen.	To threaten.
Dulden.	To bear, or endure.
Endigen.	To end.
Erben.	To inherit.
Erdichten.	To invent.
Erklären.	To explain.
Erobern.	To conquer.
Fragen.	To ask, to question.
Frühstücken.	To breakfast.
Fühlen.	To feel.
Fürchten.	To fear.
Glauben.	To believe.
Hoffen.	To hope.
Hören.	To hear.
Horchen.	To listen.
Jagen.	To hunt.
Kaufen.	To buy.
Knöpfen.	To button.
Lachen.	To laugh.
Lächeln.	To smile.
Leben.	To live.
Lehren.	To teach.
Lernen.	To learn.
Lieben.	To love.
Malen.	To paint.

OF VERBS. 65

Meinen.	To mean.
Melden.	To inform, to announce.
Mischen.	To mix.
Neiden.	To envy.
Nützen.	To profit, *or* gain.
Pflanzen.	To plant.
Prüfen.	To prove.
Rauben.	To rob.
Rechnen.	To reckon.
Reden.	To speak, *or* discourse.
Reiben.	To rub.
Reinigen.	To clean, clear, cleanse.
Richten.	To judge.
Ruhen.	To rest.
Sagen.	To say, to tell.
Schärfen.	To sharpen, to whet.
Schildern.	To portray, *or* describe.
Schwächen.	To weaken.
Seufzen.	To sigh.
Spielen.	To play.
Strafen.	To punish.
Tanzen.	To dance.
Trocknen.	To dry, to air.
Tropfen.	To drop.
Verachten.	To despise.
Verkaufen.	To sell.
Versichern.	To assure, *or* affirm.
Waschen.	To wash.
Weinen.	To weep, *or* cry.
Wetten.	To bet, to lay a wager.
Wetzen.	To whet, *or* sharpen.
Wimmern.	To lament.
Wimpern.	To wink.
Zahlen.	To pay, *or* discharge a debt.

F

Zählen.	To number, *or* count.
Zanken.	To quarrel, *or* contend.
Zeigen.	To show, *or* exhibit.
Zittern.	To tremble.
Zweifeln.	To doubt.

Irregular Verbs in Common Use.

Infinitive.	Imperfect	Past Participle.
Beißen, to bite.	biß, bit	gebissen, bitten.
Bitten, to beg, ask.	bat, bath, asked.	gebeten, asked.
Blasen, to blow.	blies, blew.	geblasen, blown.
Bleiben, to stay.	blieb, remained.	geblieben, remained.
Braten, to roast.	bratete, briet, roasted.	gebraten, roasted.
Brechen, to break.	brach, broke.	gebrochen, broken.
Brennen, to burn.	brannte, burnt.	gebrannt, burnt.
Bringen, to bring.	brachte, brought.	gebracht, brought.
Denken, to think.	dachte, thought.	gedacht, thought.
Empfangen, to receive.	empfing, received.	empfangen, received.
Essen, to eat.	aß, ate,	gegessen, eaten.
Fallen, to fall.	fiel, fell.	gefallen, fallen.
Finden, to find.	fand, found.	gefunden, found.
Fragen, to ask.	frug, asked.	gefragt, asked.
Frieren, to freeze.	fror, froze.	gefroren, frozen.
Geben, to give.	gab, gave.	gegeben, given.
Gehen, to go.	ging, went.	gegangen, gone.
Gießen, to pour.	goß, poured.	gegossen, poured.
Graben, to dig.	grub, dug.	gegraben, dug.
Haben, to have.	hatte, had.	gehabt, had.
Halten, to hold.	hielt, held.	gehalten, held.
Helfen, to know.	half, helped.	geholfen, helped.
Kennen, to know.	kannte, knew.	gekannt, known.
Kommen, to come.	kam, came.	gekommen, come.

OF VERBS.

Infinitive.	Imperfect.	Past Participle.
Können, to be able.	konnte, could.	gekonnt, been able.
Laufen, to run.	lief, ran.	gelaufen, run.
Leiden, to suffer.	litt, suffered.	gelitten, suffered.
Leihen, to lend.	lieh, lent.	geliehen, lent.
Lesen, to read.	las, read.	gelesen, read.
Liegen, to lie down.	lag, lay down.	gelegen, lain down.
Lügen, to lie.	log, lied.	gelogen, lied.
Mahlen, to grind.	mahlte, ground.	gemahlen, ground.
Nehmen, to take.	nahm, took.	genommen, taken.
Nennen, to name.	nannte, named.	genannt, named.
Pfeifen, to whistle.	pfiff, whistled.	gepfiffen, whistled.
Rathen, to advise.	rieth, advised.	gerathen, advised.
Reiben, to rub.	rieb, rubbed.	gerieben, rubbed.
Reißen, to tear.	riß, tore.	gerissen, torn.
Reiten, to ride.	ritt, rode.	geritten, ridden, rode.
Rennen, to run, rush.	rannte, ran.	gerannt, run.
Riechen, to smell.	roch, smelled.	gerochen, smelt.
Rinnen, to run, drop.	rannte, ran.	geronnen, run.
Rufen, to call out, or to cry out.	rief, called out, or cried out.	gerufen, called out, or cried out.
Schlafen, to sleep.	schlief, slept.	geschlafen, slept.
Schlagen, to beat.	schlug, beat.	geschlagen, beaten.
Schreiben, to write.	schrieb, wrote.	geschrieben, written.
Sehen, to see.	sah, saw.	gesehen, seen.
Singen, to sing.	sang, sung.	gesungen, sung.
Sinken, to sink.	sank, sunk.	gesunken, sunk.
Sitzen, to sit.	saß, sat.	gesessen, sat.
Sprechen, to speak.	sprach, spoke.	gesprochen, spoken.
Stehen, to stand.	stand, stood.	gestanden, stood.
Stehlen, to steal.	stahl, stole.	gestohlen, stolen.
Sterben, to die.	starb, died.	gestorben, dead.
Thun, to do, make.	that, did.	gethan, done.
Tragen, to carry.	trug, carried.	getragen, carried.

Infinitive.	*Imperfect.*	*Past. Participle.*
Treiben, to drive.	trieb, drove.	getrieben, driven.
Treten, to tread, step	trat, trod.	getreten, trodden.
Trügen, to deceive.	trog, deceived.	getrogen, deceived.
Trinken, to drink.	trank, drank.	getrunken, drunk.
Verbergen, to hide.	verbarg, hid.	verborgen, hidden.
Vergessen, to forget.	vergaß, forgot.	vergessen, forgotten.
Werfen, to throw.	warf, threw.	geworfen, thrown.
Wissen, to know.	wußte, knew.	gewußt, known.
Ziehen, to draw.	zog, drew.	gezogen, drawn.
Zwingen, to force.	zwang, forced.	gezwungen, forced.

VOCABULARY OF ADVERBS.

ADVERBS IN COMMON USE.

Nebenwörter.   Adverbs.

Hier, here.   Allezeit, immer, always.
Da, there.   Bald, soon, quickly.
Wo, where.   Dann, then.
Woher, wohin, whence or whereto.   Eben, nun, just now.
    Früh, early.
Oben, above.   Gestern, yesterday.
Obenauf, at the top.   Heute, to-day.
Unten, below.   Immer, ever, or always.
Unter, under.   Je, jemals, ever, always.
Nah, or nahe, near.   Jetzt, nun, now.
Fern, far.   Lange, long.
Dort, there, yonder.   Schon lange, long ago.
Dahinter, behind.   Letztens, lately.
Drinnen, drin, within.   Mehr, more.
Außen, draußen, without.   Mittags, at noon.

Morgen, to-morrow.
Nie, niemals, never.
Neulich, newly, lately.
Noch, still, yet.
Noch nicht, not yet.
Schon, already.
Seit, since.
Seither, since that time.
Stets, always, continually.
Wann? when?
Wieder, again.
Allerdings, by all means.
Gar nicht, not at all.
Gewiß, certainly.
Ja, yes.
Ja wohl, to be sure.
Kaum, hardly, scarcely.
Keineswegs, by no means.
Nein, no.
Vielleicht, perhaps.
Wahrlich, truly.
Als, wie, as, like.
Anders, otherwise.
Beinahe, nearly, almost.
Besonders, particularly.
Böse, bad, badly.
Darum, therefore.
Ganz, gar, entirely.
Genug, enough.
Gleich, like, equally.
Sogleich, gleich, directly, presently.
Hauptsächlich, chiefly.

Kurz, in short.
Mit Fleiß, on purpose.
Oberflächlich, superficially.
Rechts, rightly.
Redlich, sincerely.
Sacht, softly, gently.
Sämmtlich, all together.
Schlecht, bad, badly.
Schön, beautifully.
Sehr, very much.
So, so, thus.
So bald, as soon as.
Sonderlich, particularly, curious.
Theils, partly.
Uebel, badly, bad, ill.
Ueberaus, exceedingly.
Ungefähr, by chance.
Ungemein, uncommonly.
Unrecht, unjustly, wrong.
Völlig, fully.
Viel, much.
Warum? why?
Wie? how?
Wie viel? how much?
Wohl, gut, well.
Zugleich, together, at once.
Zum Theil, partly.
Zusammen, together.
Nirgends, nowhere.
Anderswo, elsewhere.
Allenthalben, everywhere.
Irgendwo, somewhere.

Ernsthaft, seriously. Aufrichtig, sincerely.
Scherzweise, in jest, for fun.

VOCABULARY OF PREPOSITIONS.

Prepositions Governing the Genitive.

Vorwörter.	Prepositions.
Außerhalb.	Out, without.
Diesseits.	On this side.
Innerhalb.	In, within.
Jenseit, *or* jenseits.	Beyond, on the other side.
Unweit.	Not far from.
Vermöge.	By virtue, *or* reason.
Während.	During.
Wegen.	On account of, *or* for the sake of.

Prepositions which Govern the Accusative.

Durch.	By, *or* through,
Für; Für mich.	For; For me.
Ohne; Ohne mich.	Without; Without me.
Um; Um mich.	About; About me.
Wider; Wider den Strom.	Against; Against the stream

Prepositions which Govern the Dative.

Aus, außer.	Out of, without.
Bei; Bei dem Tische.	By, near; By the table.
Entgegen.	Against towards.
Gegen=über.	Opposite to.
Mit; Mit dem Messer.	With; With the knife.
Nach; Nach mir.	After; After me.

OF CONJUNCTIONS.

Seit; Seit seinem Tode. Since; Since his death.
Von; Von dem Berge. From, of; From the mountain.
Vor; Vor der Thüre. Before; Before the door.
Zu; Zu Hause. To, at by; At home.
Zunächst. Next to.
Zuwider. Contrary, against.

Observe.— In, in, *dat.* In, into, *acc.* Auf, on, upon, *dat.* and *acc.* Hinter, behind, *dat.* and *acc.* Unter, under, among, *dat.* and *acc.* Zwischen, between, *dat.* and *acc.*

VOCABULARY OF CONJUNCTIONS.

Bindewörter.   *Conjunctions.*

Und, and. Denn, for, because.
Aber, but. Entweder, either.
Auch, also. Oder, or.
Sondern, but. Weder, neither.
Allein, but. Noch, nor.
Doch, however, yet. Zwar, indeed, however, it is
Dennoch, noch, yet, still however.   true.

The following conjunctions generally throw the verb to the end of the sentence.

Als, when, as, than. Ehe, before.
Auf daß, in order that. Falls, im Fall, in case.
Bevor, before. Indem, since, while, because.
Bis, till, until. Maßen, whereas.
Damit, in order that. Ob, whether, if.
Da, when, since, as. Obschon, obgleich, though.
Daß, that. Obwohl, wiewohl, though.
Dafern, if, in case. Wenngleich, wenn, auch, although.
Dieweil, since.

Ohngeachtet, notwithstanding.
Während, during.
Wann, when.
Wenn, if,
Wenn nur, if only, provided.

Warum, why.
Weßhalb, wherefore.
Weil, because.
Wie, how, as.
Wo, wofern, if, or in case.

Empfindungswörter.

Ach! ah! alas!
Ach wehe! who alas!
Ah! ah.
Ei! or Ey! heigh!
Halt! stop! halt!
He! or Hay! hollo! heigh!
Holla! hollo! hold!
Hui! quick! make haste!

St! schweigt! redet nicht so laut.
Sachte! Sachte!
Geh! geh! Thue was ich dir sage!
Nicht so viele Worte!
Es ist genug!
Herr N......warten Sie!
   Hier ist ein Brief für Sie.
Oh! welche Stimme!
Gott behüte euch!
Gott lob!
Was für ein Glück!
Es lebe der König!

Interjections.

Lieber! oh dear!
O! oh! O! oh!
Pfui! fy! or fye!
Siehe! look! see! behold
St! scht! hist! hush!
Weh! Wehe! woe! alas!
Weg! away!
Wohlan! well!

Hist! silence! do not speak so loud.
Gently! gently!
Go! go! do what I tell you, or do what I bid you.
Not so many words.
That's enough!
Mr. N......wait! here is a letter for you.
Oh! what a voice!
God preserve you!
God be praised!
What happiness!
Long live the king!

END OF THE VOCABULARY.

SECOND DIVISION.

Seyn, TO BE.

Seyn, TO BE, CONJUGATED WITH ADJECTIVES, &c.

PRESENT TENSE.

Ich bin sehr froh, *or* erfreuet.	I am very glad.
Du bist sehr klug.	Thou art very prudent.
Er, *or* sie ist unvorsichtig.	He *or* she is imprudent.
Es ist schmutziges Wetter.	It is dirty weather.
Wir sind fleißig.	We are diligent, industrious.
Ihr seyd faul, müßig.	You are lazy, idle.
Sie sind beschäftigt.	They, *or* you are busy.

IMPERFECT.

Ich war durstig.	I was thirsty.
Du warest hungrig.	Thou wast hungry.
Er war zufrieden.	He was contented.
Sie war zänkisch.	She was quarrelsome.
Wir waren freundlich.	We were friendly.
Ihr waret gewissenhaft.	You were conscientious.
Sie waren traurig.	They, *or* you were melancholy.

PERFECT TENSE, *or* COMPOUND OF THE PRESENT.

Ich bin krank gewesen.	I have been ill.
Du bist heiter gewesen.	Thou hast been merry.
Er ist reich gewesen.	He has been rich.
Sie ist arm gewesen.	She has been poor.

Wir sind sorgsam gewesen.   We have been careful.
Ihr seyd betrübt gewesen.   You have been afflicted.
Sie sind verdorben gewesen.   They have been corrupted.

Compound of the Imperfect.

Ich war sorglos gewesen.   I had been careless.
Du warest sparsam gewesen.   Thou hadst been saving.
Er war geizig gewesen.   He had been avaricious.

Wir waren großmüthig gewesen.   We had been generous.
Ihr waret arbeitsam gewesen.   You had been industrious.
Sie waren boshaft gewesen.   They had been malicious.

Future

Ich werde eifrig seyn.   I shall be zealous.
Du wirst fest seyn.   Thou wilt be firm.
Er wird mäßig seyn.   He will be temperate.

Wir werden vergnügt seyn.   We shall be pleased.
Ihr werdet gelehrt seyn.   You will be learned.
Sie werden unwissend seyn.   They, *or* you will be ignorant.

Compound of the Future.

Ich werde gewesen seyn.   I shall have been.
Du wirst gewesen seyn.   Thou wilt have been.
Er wird gewesen seyn.   He will have been.

Wir werden gewesen seyn.   We shall have been.
Ihr werdet gewesen seyn.   You will have been.
Sie werden gewesen seyn.   They, *or* you will have been.

Conditional.

Ich würde armselig seyn.	I should be wretched
Du würdest kühn seyn.	Thou wouldst be bold.
Er würde elend seyn.	He would be miserable.
Wir würden betrogen seyn.	We should be deceived.
Ihr würdet neidisch seyn.	You would be envious.
Sie würden bescheiden seyn.	They would be discreet.

Compound of the Conditional.

Ich würde gewesen seyn.	I should have been.
Du würdest gewesen seyn.	Thou wouldst have been.
Er würde gewesen seyn.	He would have been.
Wir würden gewesen seyn.	We should have been.
Ihr würdet gewesen seyn.	You would have been.
Sie würden gewesen seyn.	They would have been.

Imperative Mood.

Sey aufrichtig.	Be sincere.
Sey er verlassen.	Let him be forsaken.
Lasset uns aufmerksam seyn.	Let us be attentive.
Seyn Sie friedlich.	Be peaceable.
Seyn sie willkommen.	Let them be welcome.

Verneinungsweise. *Negatively.*

Present Tense.

Ich bin nicht jung.	I am not young.
Du bist nicht alt.	Thou art not old.
Er ist nicht groß.	He is not tall.
Sie ist nicht klein.	She is not short *or* little.

Wir sind nicht reich. We are not rich
Ihr seyd nicht arm. You are not poor.
Sie sind nicht dürftig. They are not indigent.

Imperfect Tense.

Ich war nicht vorsichtig. I was not prudent.
Du warest nicht unvorsichtig. Thou wast not imprudent.
Er war nicht bescheiden. He was not modest.

Wir waren nicht unverschämt. We were not impertinent.
Ihr waret nicht zänkisch. You were not quarrelsome.
Sie waren nicht ungesellig. They, *or* you were not unsociable.

Perfect Tense, *or* Compound of the Present.

Ich bin nicht sorglos gewesen. I have not been careless.
Er ist nicht fleißig gewesen. He has not been diligent.

Wir sind nicht gütig gewesen. We have not been kind.
Sie sind nicht ungerecht gewesen. They, *or* you have not been unjust.

Compound of the Imperfect.

Ich war nicht schlecht gewesen. I had not been bad.
Er war nicht böse gewesen. He had not been wicked, *or* angry.

Wir waren nicht lustig gewesen. We had not been merry.
Sie waren nicht fröhlich gewesen. They, *or* you had not been cheerful.

Future Tense.

Ich werde nicht boshaft seyn. I shall not be malicious.
Er wird nicht halsstarrig seyn. He will not be obstinate.

Wir werden nicht unmenschlich seyn.   We shall not be inhuman.
Sie werden nicht menschlich seyn.   They, *or* you will not be humane.

Conditional.

Ich würde nicht stolz seyn.   I should not be proud.
Er würde nicht milde seyn.   He would not be mild.

Wir würden nicht häßlich seyn.   We should not be ugly.
Sie würden nicht schön seyn.   They, *or* you would not be beautiful.

Verneinungs= und frage=weise.   *Negatively and Interrogatively.*

Present Tense.

Bin ich nicht blaß?   Am I not pale?
Ist sie nicht hübsch?   Is she not pretty?

Sind wir nicht sterblich?   Are we not mortal?
Sind Sie nicht glücklich?   Are you not happy?
Sind sie nicht unglücklich?   Are they not unhappy?

Imperfect Tense.

War ich nicht sanft?   Was I not affable, mild?
Warest du nicht stolz?   Wast thou not proud?
War er nicht schwach?   Was he not weak?

Waren wir nicht fest?   Were we not firm?
Waren Sie nicht pünktlich?   Were you not punctual?
Waren sie nicht billig?   Were they not reasonable?

Compound of the Present.

Bin ich nicht dumm gewesen?   Have I not been stupid?
Bist du nicht närrisch gewesen?   Hast thou not been foolish?
Ist er nicht weise gewesen?   Has he not been wise?

Sind wir nicht höflich gewesen?	Have we not been polite, *or* civil?
Sind Sie nicht betrogen gewesen?	Have you not been deceived?
Sind sie nicht neidisch gewesen?	Have they not been envious?

COMPOUND OF THE IMPERFECT.

War ich nicht betrübt gewesen?	Had I not been afflicted?
War er nicht niedergeschlagen gewesen?	Had he not been dejected?
Waren wir nicht krank gewesen?	Had we not been ill?
Waren sie nicht eitel gewesen?	Had they not been vain?

FUTURE TENSE.

Werde ich nicht matt seyn?	Shall I not be faint?
Wird er nicht grausam seyn?	Will he not be cruel?
Werden wir nicht gesund seyn?	Shall we not be healthy?
Werden sie nicht tapfer seyn?	Will they not be brave?

CONDITIONAL.

Würde ich nicht herzhaft seyn?	Should I not be courageous?
Würde er nicht strafbar seyn?	Would he not be punishable?
Würden wir nicht fröhlich seyn?	Should we not be cheerful?
Würden sie nicht unartig seyn?	Would they not be perverse?

Frageweise und verneinungsweise, u. s. w.	*Interrogatively and Negatively,* &c.
Bist du glücklich?	Art thou happy?
Nein, ich bin sehr unglücklich.	No, I am very unhappy.
Ich bin sehr traurig.	I am very gloomy.
Ich bin sehr müde.	I am very tired.

INTERROGATIVELY AND NEGATIVELY, &c.

Wo sind Sie gewesen?	Where have you been?
Ich bin bei meiner Tante gewesen.	I have been to my aunt's.
Wir sind in London gewesen.	We have been to London.
Und wo sind Sie gewesen?	And where have you been?
Ich bin bei dem Buchhändler gewesen.	I have been to the bookseller's.
Wo ist Ihr Vater gewesen?	Where has your father been?
Er ist in Paris gewesen.	He has been to Paris.
Mein Bruder ist in Amsterdam gewesen.	My brother has been in Amsterdam.
Wo ist Ihre Schwester gewesen?	Where has your sister been?
Sie ist zu Hause gewesen.	She has been home.
Sind nicht die Kinder im Hause?	Are not the children in the house?
Nein, sie sind in der Schule.	No, they are in the school.
Ich bin selbst in der Schule gewesen.	I have been into the school myself.
Waren Sie nicht böse?	Were you not angry?
Nein, ich war gütig.	No, I was kind.
Die Kinder waren nicht halsstarrig.	The children were not obstinate.
Sie waren sehr gut.	They were very good.

Seyn, TO BE, WITH VARIOUS PARTS OF SPEECH.

Wer ist da?	Who is there?
Ich bin es; er ist es.	It is I; it is he.
Wo sind Sie?	Where are you?
Ich bin hier.	I am here.
Sind Sie in Deutschland gewesen?	Have you been to Germany?
Ich bin nicht da gewesen.	I have not been there.
Sind Sie ein Engländer?	Are you an Englishman?
Nein, ich bin ein Deutscher.	No, I am a German.

Ist Herr Schmidt zu Hause? | Is Mr. Schmidt at home?
Nein, er ist nicht zu Hause. | No, he is not at home.
Es würde mir lieb gewesen seyn, ihn zu sehen. | I should have been glad to see him.
Er war so eben auf dem Comptoir. | He was just now in the counting-house.
Er ist vielleicht in seiner Stube. | He is perhaps in his room.
Man sagte mir, daß Sie nicht zu Hause wären. | I was told that you were not at home.
Wo sind die Kleinen? | Where are the little ones?
Sie sind in den Garten. | They are in the garden.
Sind Sie gestern bei Frau von R......gewesen? | Where you at Lady R.'s yesterday?
Schon länger als ein halbes Jahr bin ich nicht bei ihr (da) gewesen. | It is now more than six months since I was there.
Verzeihen Sie, ich komme in einem Augenblick wieder. | Pardon me, Sir, I shall be back again in a moment.

Haben, TO HAVE.

Haben, TO HAVE, CONJUGATED WITH NOUNS, &c.

PRESENT TENSE.

Ich habe einen Rock. | I have a coat.
Du hast einen Hut. | Thou hast a hat.
Er hat eine Weste. | He has a waistcoat.

Wir haben Strümpfe. | We have stockings.
Ihr habet Beinkleider. | You have small-clothes.
Sie haben Schuhe. | They, *or* you have shoes.

IMPERFECT TENSE.

Ich hatte eine Taschenuhr. | I had a watch.
Du hattest ein Halstuch. | Thou hadst a cravat.
Er hatte ein Halsband. | He had a collar.

WITH VARIOUS NOUNS.

Wir hatten Strumpfbänder.   We had garters.
Ihr hattet Schnallen.   You had buckles.
Sie hatten Stiefel.   They, *or* you had boots.

PERFECT, OR COMPOUND OF THE IMPERFECT.

Ich habe einen Kamm gehabt.   I have had a comb.
Du hast eine Mütze gehabt.   Thou hast had a cap.
Er hat einen Stock gehabt.   He has had a stick.

Wir haben Geld gehabt.   We have had money.
Ihr habet Geld genug gehabt.   You have had money enough.
Sie haben Juwelen gehabt.   They, *or* you have had jewels.

PLUPERFECT OR COMPOUND OF THE IMPERFECT.

Ich hatte Thee gehabt.   I had had tea.
Du hattest Caffee gehabt.   Thou hadst had coffee.
Er hatte Butterbrod gehabt, oder Brod und Butter.   He had had bread and butter.

Wir hatten Milch gehabt.   We had had milk.
Ihr hattet Rahm gehabt.   You had had cream.
Sie hatten Zucker gehabt.   They, *or* you had had sugar.

FUTURE TENSE.

Ich werde Schinken haben.   I shall have some ham.
Du wirst Eier haben.   Thou wilt have some eggs.
Er wird Zunge haben.   He will have some tongue.

Wir werden Hutzucker haben.   We shall have some loaf sugar.

Ihr werdet Honig haben.   You will have some honey.
Sie werden Chocolade haben.   They will have chocolate.

Compound of the Future.

Ich werde Zeit gehabt haben.	I shall have had time.
Er wird Gedulb gehabt haben.	He will have had patience.
Wir werden Vergnügen gehabt haben.	We shall have had pleasure.
Sie werden Muth gehabt haben.	They, *or* you will have had courage.

Conditional.

Ich würde Freunde haben.	I should have friends.
Du würdest Feinde haben.	Thou wouldst have enemies.
Er würde Bedienten haben.	He would have servants.
Wir würden Vorgesetzte haben.	We should have superiors.
Ihr würdet Niedrigere haben.	You would have inferiors.
Sie würden Gleiche haben.	They would have equals.

Compound of the Conditional.

Ich würde Kinder gehabt haben.	I should have had children.
Er würde Gedulb gehabt haben.	He would have had patience.
Wir würden Verwandte gehabt haben.	We should have had relations.
Ihr würdet Beistand gehabt haben.	You would have had assistance.
Sie würden ein Geschenk gehabt haben.	They, *or* you would have had a present.

Frageweise.   *Interrogatively*

Present Tense.

Habe ich einen Bleistift?	Have I a pencil?
Hast du eine Schiefertafel?	Hast thou a slate?
Hat er ein Federmesser?	Has he a pen-knife.

WITH VARIOUS NOUNS.

Haben wir Dinte?   Have we any ink?
Habet ihr Papier?   Have you any paper?
Haben Sie Federn?   Have you any pens?
Haben sie Siegellack?   Have they any sealing-wax?

IMPERFECT TENSE.

Hatte ich Ihr Buch?   Had I your book?
Hattest du mein Dintenfaß?   Hadst thou my inkstand?
Hatte er ein Schreibbuch?   Had he a copy-book?

Hatten wir Ihr Siegel?   Had we your seal?
Hattet ihr eine Oblate?   Had you a wafer?
Hatten sie ein Buch Papier?   Had they a quire of paper?

PERFECT, OR COMPOUND OF THE PRESENT.

Habe ich Silber gehabt?   Have I had some silver?
Hast du Kupfer gehabt?   Hast thou had any copper?
Hat er Eisen gehabt?   Has he had some iron?

Haben wir Gold gehabt?   Have we had any gold?
Habet ihr Blei gehabt?   Have you had any lead?
Haben sie Messing gehabt?   Have they had any brass?

PLUPERFECT, OR COMPOUND OF THE IMPERFECT.

Hattest du Blech gehabt?   Hadst thou had tin?
Hatte er einen Stuhl gehabt?   Had he had a chair?

Hatten wir ein Messer gehabt?   Had we had a knife?
Hatten sie eine Gabel gehabt?   Had they had a fork?

FUTURE TENSE.

Werde ich Fleisch haben?   Shall I have some meat?
Wirst du Rindfleisch haben?   Wilt thou have some beef?
Wird er Hammelfleisch haben?   Will he have some mutton?

Werden wir Kalbfleisch haben?	Shall we have some veal?
Werdet ihr Lammfleisch haben?	Shall you have any lamb?
Werden sie Schweinefleisch haben?	Will they have some pork?

COMPOUND OF THE FUTURE.

Werde ich gehabt haben?	Shall I have had?
Wirst du gehabt haben?	Wilt thou have had?
Wird er gehabt haben?	Will he have had?
Werden wir gehabt haben?	Shall we have had?
Werdet ihr gehabt haben?	Shall you have had?
Werden sie gehabt haben?	Will they have had?

CONDITIONAL.

Würde ich eine Antwort haben?	Should I have an answer?
Würdest du einen Nutzen haben?	Wouldst thou have a profit?
Würde er Waaren haben?	Would he have goods?
Würden wir Reichthümer haben?	Should we have riches?
Würdet ihr Obst haben?	Would you have some fruit?
Würden sie Lichter haben?	Would they have candles?

COMPOUND OF THE CONDITIONAL.

Würde ich gehabt haben?	Should I have had?
Würde er gehabt haben?	Would he have had?
Würden wir gehabt haben?	Should we have had?
Würden sie gehabt haben?	Would they have had?

Verneinungsweise. *Negatively.*

PRESENT TENSE.

Ich habe keinen Schawl.	I have no shawl.
Du hast keinen Schleier.	Thou hast no veil.
Sie hat keinen Hut.	She has no bonnet.

Wir haben keinen Muff. — We have no muff.
Sie haben keine Strumpfbänder. — They have no garters.

IMPERFECT.

Ich hatte keine Handschuhe. — I had no gloves.
Du hattest kein Taschentuch. — Thou hadst no handkerchief.
Sie hatte keine Armbänder. — She had no bracelets.

Wir hatten keinen Fächer. — We had no fan.
Ihr hattet keine Juwelen. — You had no jewels.
Sie hatten keinen Kamm. — They, *or* you had no comb.

PERFECT, OR COMPOUND OF THE PRESENT.

Ich habe kein Band gehabt. — I have had no ribbon.
Du hast keine Schnürbrust gehabt. — Thou hast had no stays.
Sie hat kein Schnürband gehabt. — She has had no lace.

Wir haben keine Bänder gehabt. — We have had no ribbons.
Ihr habet keinen Sonnenschirm gehabt. — You have had no parasol.
Sie haben keinen Regenschirm gehabt. — They, *or* you have had no umbrella.

PLUPERFECT, OR COMPOUND OF THE IMPERFECT.

Ich hatte keine Schürze gehabt. — I had had no apron.
Sie hatte keinen Ohrring gehabt. — She had had no ear-ring.

Wir hatten keine Stecknadeln gehabt. — We had had no pins.
Sie hatten keine Nähnadeln gehabt. — They, *or* you had had no needles.

FUTURE TENSE.

Ich werde keinen Fingerhut haben. — I shall have no thimble.
Du wirst keinen Faden haben. — Thou wilt have no thread.
Sie wird keinen Unterrock haben. — She will have no petticoat.

Wir werden keinen Diamant haben. — We shall have no diamond.
Sie werden keinen Ring haben. — They will have no ring.

CONDITIONAL.

Ich würde keine Bedienten haben. — I should have no servants.
Du würdest keine Mägde haben. — Thou wouldst have no *maid* servants.
Er würde keinen Kutscher haben. — He would have no coachman.

Wir würden keinen Lohn haben. — We should have no wages.
Sie würden keine Kutsche haben. — You would have no coach.
Sie würden keine Pferde haben. — They would have no horses.

Verneinungs- und fragweise. — *Negatively and interrogativly.*

PRESENT TENSE.

Habe ich keine Kleidung? — Have I no dress?
Hast du keinen Gehalt? — Hast thou no salary?
Hat er keine Diamanten? — Has he no diamonds?

Haben wir keine Messer? — Have we no knives?
Habet ihr keine Gabeln? — Have you no forks?
Haben sie keine Löffel? — Have they no spoons?

IMPERFECT.

Hattest du keinen Teller? — Hadst thou no plate?
Hatte er keine Schüssel? — Had he no dish?

Hatten wir keine Caraffine? — Had we no decanter?
Hatten sie kein Weinglas? — Had they no wine-glass?

Perfect, or Compound of the Present.

Habe ich keinen Wein gehabt?	Have I had no wine?
Hast du keinen Korkzieher gehabt?	Hast thou had no corkscrew?
Hat er keinen Becher gehabt?	Has he had no tumbler?
Haben wir keinen Senftopf gehabt?	Have we had no mustard-pot?
Habet ihr keinen Krug gehabt?	Have you had no jug?
Haben sie kein Salzfaß gehabt?	Have they had no salt-cellar?

Pluperfect, or Compound of the Imperfect.

Hatte ich keine Suppe gehabt?	Had I had no soup?
Hattest du keinen Speck gehabt?	Hadst thou had no bacon?
Hatte er keinen Schinken gehabt?	Had he had no ham?
Hatten wir keine Pastete gehabt?	Had we had no pie?
Hattet ihr keinen Käse gehabt?	Had you had no cheese?
Hatten sie keine Kartoffeln gehabt?	Had they had no potatoes?

Future Tense.

Werde ich keinen Fisch haben?	Shall I have no fish?
Wirst du keinen Lachs haben?	Wilt thou have no salmon?
Wird er keine Makrele haben?	Will he have no mackerel?
Werden wir keinen Steinfisch, or Kabeljau haben?	Shall we have no cod-fish?
Werdet ihr kein Wildpret haben?	Shall you have no game?
Werden sie keinen Fasan haben?	Will they have oo pheasant?

Conditional.

Würdest du keine Gans haben?	Wouldst thou have no goose?
Würde er keine Ente haben?	Would he have no duck?

Würden wir keinen Truthahn haben?	Should we have no turkey?
Würdet ihr keinen Hasen haben?	Would you have no hare?
Würden sie kein Küchlein haben?	Would they have no chicken?

The Future,

Or rather Present with Sollen *and* Wollen.

Soll ich Wein haben?	Shall I have some wine?
Willst du Wasser haben?	Wilt thou have some water?
Nein, ich will Bier haben.	No, I will have some beer.
Soll er ein Glas Portwein haben?	Shall he have a glass of Port wine?
Nein, er wird ein Glas Porter trinken.	No, he will drink a glass of porter.
Sollen wir Xereswein haben?	Shall we have some sherry?
Wollet ihr Rheinwein haben?	Will you have some Hock?
Ich danke Ihnen, ich will ein wenig Bordeaux trinken.	No, thank you, I will drink a little claret.
Wollen Sie Madeirawein haben?	Will you have some Madeira?
Sie sollen Burgunderwein haben.	You shall have some Burgundy wine.
Sie sollen weißen Wein haben.	They shall have some white wine.
Sie wollen ihn nicht trinken.	They will not drink it.
Was wollen Sie, Herr N.?	What will you take Mr. N.?
Ich will ein Glas Brantwein und Wasser haben.	I will take a glass of brandy and water.
Wollen Sie Zucker haben?	Will you take some sugar?
Ein wenig.	A little, if you please.
Sollte ich Rum haben?	Should I have some rum?
Er wollte Limonade haben.	He would have lemonade.

IMPERSONAL VERBS.

Es regnet.	It rains.
Es hagelt.	It hails.
Es schneiet.	It snows.
Es friert.	It freezes.
Es thauet.	It thaws.
Es wehet.	It blows.
Es donnert.	It thunders.
Es blitzet.	It lightens.
Es ist frostig.	It is frosty.
Es ist stürmisch.	It is stormy.
Es ist wolkig.	It is cloudy.
Es ist klar.	It is clear.
Es ist nebelig.	It is foggy.
Es ist naß.	It is wet.
Es ist trocken.	It is dry.
Es ist regnicht.	It is rainy.
Es ist windig.	It is windy.
Es ist warm.	It is warm.
Es ist heiß.	It is hot.
Es ist kalt.	It is cold.
Es ist hell.	It is light.
Es ist Tageslicht.	It is daylight.
Es ist dunkel.	It is dark.
Es taget.	It dawns.
Es ist schönes Wetter.	It is fine weather.
Es ist schlechtes Wetter.	It is bad weather.
Es ist schmutzig, or kothig.	It is dirty.
Es ist veränderliches Wetter.	It is changeable weather.

THIRD DIVISION.

FAMILIAR PHRASES.

Nützliche Bitten.   *Useful Requests.*

Geben Sie mir, *or* Gieb mir   *Give me some*

Haben Sie die Güte und geben Sie mir	ein wenig, *or* etwas		Have the goodness to give me a little	*or some*		if you please.
		Brot, *or* Brod.			bread,	
		Wein.			wine,	
		Bier.			beer,	
		Fleisch.			meat,	
		Rindfleisch.			beef,	
		Hammelfleisch.			mutton,	
		Kalbfleisch.			veal,	
		Lammfleisch.			lamb,	
		Schweinfleisch.			pork,	
		Speck.			bacon,	
		Schinken.			ham,	
		Suppe.			soup,	
		Fisch.			fish,	

Observe.—The phrases and sentences in this, and the following pages, being applicable to the names of many things in common use, they will enable the traveller, to ask in German, for almost every thing he may require.

Bringen Sie mir, or Bring mir   Bring me

Seyn Sie so gut und bringen Sie mir {
  ein Messer — a knife,
  eine Gabel — a fork,
  einen Löffel — a spoon,
  einen Teller — a plate,
  eine Schüssel — a dish,
  ein Glas — a glass,
  ein Weinglas — a wine-glass,
  einen Becher — a tumbler,
  eine Serviette — a napkin,
  die Caraffine — the decanter,
  den Senftopf — the mustard-pot,
  das Essigfläschchen — the vinegar-cruet,
  den Korkzieher — the corkscrew,
  einen Krug — a jug, or, pitcher,
}

wenn es Ihnen beliebt, or *
wenn es Ihnen gefällig ist.

Have the kindness to bring me ... if you please.

* Although the author has here given the expressions which correspond to the English *if you please*, yet this mode of speaking is not so common in German as in English.

Leihen Sie mir   Lend me

Wollen Sie mir gefälligst {
  ein Buch — a book,
  eine Feder — a pen,
  ein Federmesser — a pen-knife,
  Dinte, or Tinte — some ink,
  ein Tintenfaß — an inkstand,
  eine Schiefertafel — a slate.
  einen Bleistift — a lead pencil,
  einen Griffel — a slate pencil,
  eine Oblate — a wafer,
  ein Siegel — a seal,
  Papier — some paper,
  Siegellack — some sealing-wax,
}

leihen.

Will you lend me ... if you please.

Schicken Sie mir, or Schicke mir   Send me

Pfeffer	some pepper.
Salz	— salt.
Senf	— mustard.
Essig	— vinegar.
Oel	— oil.
Kartoffeln	— potatoes.
Erbsen	— peas.
Weiße Rüben	— turnips.
Blumenkohl	— cauliflower.
Kohl	— cabbage.
Zwiebeln	— onions.
Radiese	— radishes.
Gurken	— cucumbers.
Salat	— salad.
Petersilie	— parsley.

(Soll ich Ihnen etwas ... schicken?)   (Shall I send you)

Wollen Sie ein wenig   *Will you take a little*

Suppe	soup?
Pfeffer	pepper?
Salz	salt?
Senf	mustard?
Essig	vinegar?
Oel	Oil?
Brühe	sauce?
Fleischbrühe	broth?

(haben?)

Wenn ich bitten darf.   If you please.

Ist Ihnen etwas   *Will you take some*

Lachs, or Salm	salmon?
Makrele	mackerel?
Steinbütte	turbot?

(gefällig?)

Ist Ihnen etwas   Will you take some
  Kabeljau   codfish?
  Scholle   sole?
  Hecht   *gefällig?* pike, *or* jack?
  Forelle   trout?
  Aal   eel?
Wenn Sie so gut seyn wollen.   If you please.

Ist Ihnen gefällig ein Glas   Will you take a glass
  Bier zu trinken   of beer?
  Porter   of porter?
  Wein   of wine?
  Portwein   *trinken?*   of port?
  Xereswein   of sherry?
  Madeirawein   of madeira?
  Bordeaux   of claret?
  Champagner   of champagne?

(Wollen Sie ein Glas)

Ich habe die Ehre zu Ihrer   I have the honour to drink
  Gesundheit zu trinken.   your health.

    Befehlen, u.s.w.   *To command, &c.*
Hohlen Sie mir, *or* hohle mir   Fetch, *or* go for
  mein Halstuch, *n.*   my cravat.
  meinen Hut, *m.*   my hat.
  meine Tasche, *f.*   my pocket.
  meinen Ueberrock, *m.*   my great-coat.
  meinen Mantel, *m.*   my cloak.
  meine Strümpfe, *m.*   my stockings.
  meine Schuhe, *m.*   my shoes.
  meine Pantoffel, *m.*   my slippers.
  meine Stiefel, *m.*   my boots.

FAMILIAR PHRASES.

Laſſen Sie ... . hohlen. Send for some
  Milch   milk.
  Kartoffeln   potatoes.
  Erbſen   peas.
  Weiße Rüben   turnips.
  Obſt   fruit.
  Aepfel   apples.
  Erdbeeren   strawberries.
  Himbeeren   raspberries.
  Stachelbeeren   gooseberries.
  Johannisbeeren   currants.
  Trauben   grapes.
  Apfelſinen   oranges.
Was ſoll ich Ihnen ſchicken? What shall I send you?

(Wollen Sie ... hohlen laſſen?)
(Will you send for some ...)

AFFIRMATIVE PHRASES.

Ich kenne ihn.	I know him.
Ich kenne ſie.	I know her, *or* them.
Ich weiß es.	I know it.
Er kennet mich.	He knows me.
Es iſt wahr.	It is true.
Sie kennen uns.	They know us.
Ich glaube, ja.	I believe so.
Es iſt ſo.	It is so.
Sie haben Recht.	You are right.
Er hat Unrecht.	He is wrong.
Ich ſage, ja.	I say yes.
Ich glaube es.	I believe it.
Wir denken ſo.	We think so.
Ich bin deſſen gewiß.	I am certain of it.
Er hatte unrecht.	He was wrong.
Ich weiß es zuverläſſig.	I know it positively.
Er iſt zu Hauſe.	He is at home.

Er ist noch im Bette.	He is still in bed.
Sie schläft noch.	She is still asleep.
Er ist aufgestanden.	He is up.
Es ist Zeit aufzustehen.	It is time to get up.
Ich bin angekleidet.	I am dressed.
Es ist sehr spät.	It is very late.
Es ist noch frühe.	It is still early.
Ich bin krank.	I am ill.
Ich bedaure Sie.	I pity you.
Wir haben gefrühstückt.	We have breakfasted.
Ich habe Ihnen etwas zu sagen.	I have something to tell you.
Wir werden Morgen aufs Land gehen.	We shall go into the country to-morrow.
Ich bin frühe ausgegangen.	I went out early.
Ich kam spät zurück.	I came back late.
Ich bin ermüdet, or müde.	I am fatigued, or tired.
Das thut mir leid.	I am sorry for it.
Er hat den Schnupfen.	He has a cold.
Ich bin erkältet.	I have a cold.
Ich habe mich erkältet.	I have caught a cold.
Ich habe Kopfweh.	I have the head ache.
Ich habe einen Husten.	I have a cough.
Ich habe Zahnschmerzen.	I have the tooth ache.
Mir thut der Zahn sehr wehe.	My tooth aches very much.
Ich will zu Bette gehen.	I will go to bed.
Ich bin schläferig.	I am sleepy.
Mir ist sehr kalt, mich friert's sehr, or es friert mich sehr.	I am very cold.
Mir ist sehr warm.	I am very warm.
Es ist Zeit abzureisen.	It is time to set off.
Der Wagen ist da, or hier.	The carriage is come.
Der Wagen ist bereit.	The carriage is ready.
Die Pferde sind angespannt.	The horses are to.
Die Pferde sind gut.	The horses are good.

Sie sind sehr müde.	They are very tired.
Wir müssen hier anhalten.	We must stop here.
Der Kutscher ist betrunken.	The coachman is drunk.
Der Fuhrmann ist besoffen, *or* berauscht.	The driver is tipsy, *or* in liquor.
Ich war zu Pferde.	I was on horseback.
Sie waren zu Fuße.	They were on foot.
Ich werde übermorgen nach London gehen.	I shall go to London the day after to-morrow.
Ich werde bald wieder kommen.	I shall soon return.
Es gefällt mir, dir, ihm, u. s. w.	It pleases me, thee, him, &c.
Es gebühret mir.	It becomes me.
Es fehlt mir, *or* mir fehlt.	I want.
Es kommt mir vor.	It seems to me, it reminds me.
Es bekommt mir.	It agrees with me.
Es scheint mir, *or* mir scheint es.	It seems to me.
Es ist mir Angst, mir ist Angst.	I am afraid.
Es ist mir wohl, mir ist wohl.	I am well.
Es jammert, *or* dauert mich.	It grieves me.
Es betrübet mich.	It afflicts me.
Es freuet mich.	It rejoices me, *or* I rejoice.
Es reuet mich.	I repent, *or* it repents me.
Es wundert mich.	It surprises me.
Es verdrießt mich.	It vexes me.
Es hungert mich, *or* mich hungert.	I am hungry.
Es durstet mich, *or* mich durstet.	I am thirsty.
Es hungert dich.	Thou art hungry.
Es durstet dich.	Thou art thirsty.
Es hungert uns.	We are hungry.
Es durstet sie.	They are thirsty.
Es schläfert mich.	I am sleepy.
Es schläfert dich.	Thou art sleepy.
Es schläfert uns.	We are sleepy.

Verneinende Redensarten.	Negative Phrases.
Ich kannte ihn nicht.	I did not know him.
Ich habe ihn nicht gesehen.	I have not seen him.
Er ist es nicht gewesen.	It was not he.
Er ist es nicht.	It is not he.
Ich bin es nicht.	It is not I.
Du bist es nicht.	It is not thou.
Sie ist es nicht.	It is not she.
Wir sind es nicht,	It is not we.
Ihr seyd es nicht.	It is not you.
Sie sind es nicht.	It is not they, *or* you.
Das ist nicht wahr.	That is not true.
Niemand sagt es.	Nobody says so.
Ich sage nichts.	I say nothing.
Ich sage nein.	I say no.
Ich thue nichts.	I am doing nothing.
Er ist nicht da.	He is not there.
Es ist niemand da.	There is nobody.
Ich sah niemand.	I saw nobody.
Sie sahen ihn nie.	You never saw him.
Sie wissen nichts.	You know nothing.
Sie haben gar nicht gelesen.	You have not read at all.
Er hat seine Lection nicht gelernt.	He has not learned his lesson.
Ich sagte dies nicht.	I did not say that.
Sie haben heute nicht studirt.	You have not studied to-day
Ich war nicht in der Stadt.	I was not in town.
Er ist nicht zu Hause.	He is not at home.
Ich glaube es nicht.	I do not believe it.
Sagen Sie kein Wort.	Don't say a word.
Ich höre ihm nicht zu.	I do not listen to him, *or* I don't hear him.
Ich horche nicht.	I am not listening.

Wir sind nicht immer so munter.	We are not always so cheerful.
Sie wird nicht undankbar seyn.	She will not be ungrateful.
Wir verlangen nichts.	We ask for, *or* want nothing.
Er will nichts haben.	He will have nothing.
Er will nicht zu Ihnen gehen.	He will not go to your house.
Wir wollen nicht zu Ihnen gehen.	We will not go to your house.
Sie haben nicht Unrecht.	You are not in the wrong.
Er hat nicht Recht.	He is not right.
Der Tisch ist nicht gedeckt.	The table is not laid.
Das Mittagessen ist nicht fertig *or* bereit.	Dinner is not ready (*prepared*).
Das Abendessen ist noch nicht fertig, *or* bereitet.	Supper is not yet ready.
Ich esse nie Fleisch des Abends.	I never eat meat at night.
Der Wagen ist noch nicht angekommen.	The carriage is not yet come.
Die Pferde sind noch nicht angekommen.	The horses are not yet come.
Es ist noch nicht Zeit abzureisen.	It is not yet time to set off.
Die Pferde sind nicht gut.	The horses are not good.
Ich weiß nicht wie viel Uhr es ist.	I do not know what o'clock it is.
Ich weiß die Stunde der Abreise nicht.	I do not know the time for setting off.
Ich habe nicht gehört.	I have not heard.
Ich hatte nicht verstanden.	I did not understand.
Ich weiß den Namen dieses Landes nicht.	I do not know the name of this country.
Sie gehen nicht spazieren.	They are not going to walk.
Ich bin nicht hungrig.	I am not hungry.
Ich auch nicht.	Nor I either.
Ich will kein Brod.	I won't have any bread.

Ich habe keinen Appetit. I have no appetite.
Er will keinen Wein. He will have no wine.
Ich bin nicht durstig. I am not thirsty.
Ich gehe nirgends hin. I am going no where.
Ich bin nicht schläferig. I am not sleepy.
Ich bin nicht müde. I am not tired.
Ich will nicht zu Bette gehen. I will not go to bed.
Mir ist nicht warm. I am not warm.
Es ist nicht sehr warm. It is not very warm.
Ich bin etwas unpäßlich. I am rather indisposed.
Er löschte das Licht nicht aus. He did not put out or extinguish the candle.

Er hat seine Arbeit nicht geendigt. He has not finished his work.
Sie haben den Satz nicht bewiesen. You have not demonstrated the proposition.

Fragende Redensarten. *Interrogative Phrases.*

Was ist es für Wetter? How is the weather?
Scheint die Sonne? Does the sun shine?
Ist es windig? Is it windy?
Staubet es? Is it dusty?
Ist es schmutzig? Is it dirty?
Ist es schmutzig auf der Straße? Is it dirty in the street?
Ist es trocken auf den Straßen? Is it dry in the streets?
Wird es regnen? Will it rain?
Hat es geregnet? Has it rained?
Schneiet es? Does it snow?
Nebelt es? Is it foggy?
Hat es geschneiet? Has it snowed?
Ist es warm? Is it warm?
Ist Ihnen warm? Are you warm?
Was sagen Sie? What do you say?

Was giebt es?	What is the matter?
Wer ist es?	Who is it?
Wer ist dieser?	Who is this?
Wer klopft?	Who knocks, *or* is knocking?
Wer ruft mich?	Who calls me?
Was machen Sie?	What are you doing?
Was wollen Sie?	What do you want?
Was verlangen Sie?	What do you wish?
Wo sind Sie?	Where are you?
Wo ist er?	Where is he?
Was macht er?	What is he doing?
Was machen sie?	What are they doing?
Wo gehen Sie hin?	Where are you going?
Wo gehen wir hin?	Where are we going?
Wohin wollen Sie gehen?	Where will you go to?
Wo gehen wir hin?	Where are we going?
Wo sollen wir gehen?	Where shall we go?
Wo wollen Sie hingehen?	Where will you go to?
Wo kommen Sie her?	Where do you come from?
Sind Sie in Deutschland gewesen?	Have you been in Germany?
Gehen Sie nach London?	Are you going to London?
Wo sind Sie gewesen?	Where have you been?
Wie befinden Sie sich?	How do you do, Sir?
Wie befindet sich Ihr Herr Bruder?	How is your brother? *or* how does your brother do.
Wie befinden sich Ihr Herr Vater und Ihre Frau Mutter?	How are your father and mother?
Wie befindet sich Ihre Mamsell Schwester?	How does your sister do?
Ist sie zu Hause?	Is she at home?
Haben Sie sie gesehen?	Have you seen her?
Haben Sie sie erwartet?	Did you expect her?
Haben Sie ihn gesehen?	Have you seen him?

Haben Sie sie angetroffen?	Have you met them?
Haben Sie mit ihm gesprochen?	Have you spoken to him?
Haben Sie mit ihnen gesprochen?	Have you spoken to them?
Haben Sie mit ihr getanzt?	Have you danced with her?
Waren Sie nicht auf dem Balle gewesen?	Had you not been to the ball?
Werde ich das Vergnügen haben Sie morgen zu sehen?	Shall I have the pleasure of seeing you to-morrow?
Werden Sie eine zahlreiche Gesellschaft haben?	Shall you have a large party? *or* much company?
Werden wir hingehen können?	Shall we be able to go there?
Werden wir Zeit dazu haben?	Shall we have time for it?
Warum kommen Sie so spät?	Why do you come so late?
Wie kommt es daß Sie heute so viele Geschäfte haben?	How is it that you have so much business to-day?
Wer hat es Ihnen gesagt?	Who told you so?
Wer hat Ihnen das gesagt?	Who told you that?
Wer hat das gethan?	Who has done that?
Was ist das?	What is that?
Wessen Kleid ist dieses?	Whose coat is this?
Wem gehört dieses Kleid?	To whom does this coat belong?
Wem haben Sie es gegeben?	To whom have you given it?
Mit wem haben Sie gesprochen?	To whom did you speak?
Von wem haben Sie es gehöret?	From whom did you hear it?
Wen haben Sie eingeladen?	Whom have you invited?
Zu wem gehn Sie?	To whose house are you going?
Von wem kommen Sie?	From whose house do you come?
Bei wem sind Sie gewesen?	At whose house have you been?
Was für ein Buch werden wir morgen lesen?	What book shall we read to-morrow?

Was für eine Farbe ziehen Sie vor?	What color do you prefer?
Welcher Farbe geben Sie den Vorzug?	To which color do you give the preference?
Welche ziehen Sie vor, die blauen, oder die gelben?	Which do you prefer, the blues, or yellows?
Hier sind zwei Bleistifte, m.	Here are two pencils.
Welchen wollen Sie haben?	Which will you have?
Hier sind zwei Federn, f.	Here are two pens.
Welche wollen Sie nehmen?	Which will you take?
Was für Bücher hat er gekauft?	What books has he bought?
Welchen geben Sie den Vorzug?	To which do you give the preference?
Welches von diesen beiden Gemälten gefällt Ihnen am besten?	Which of these two pictures do you prefer, *or* do you like best?
Wer sind diese Herren, mit welchen Sie so eben sprachen?	Who are those gentlemen with whom you were just speaking?
Sprechen Sie im Ernst?	Are you speaking in earnest?
Sprechen Sie Deutsch?	Do you speak German?
Haben Sie mich verstanden?	Did you understand me?
Verstehen Sie mich?	Do you understand me?
Habe ich richtig ausgesprochen?	Have I pronounced correctly?
Sind Sie in Deutschland gewesen?	Have you been in Germany?
Was denken Sie von der deutschen Sprache?	What do you think of the German language?
Verstehen Sie was Sie lesen?	Do you understand what you read?
Wie lange haben Sie gelernt?	How long have you learnt?
Wie nennen Sie das auf Deutsch?	What do you call that in German?

Wollen Sie frühstücken?	Will you breakfast?
Wollen Sie Butterbrod?	Will you have some bread and butter?
Wollen Sie eine Tasse Thee?	Will you take a cup of tea?
Ist das Mittagsessen fertig, or bereit?	Is dinner ready? or is dinner prepared?
Ist das Abendessen fertig?	Is supper ready?
Wollen Sie den Flügel eines Küchlein?	Will you have the wing of a chicken?
Wollen Sie Wein?	Will you have some wine?
Wollen Sie ein Glas Wein und Wasser?	Will you have a glass of wine and water?
Ist der Wagen angekommen?	Is the carriage come?
Sind die Pferde angekommen?	Are the horses come?
Wann werden wir abreisen?	When shall we set off?
Welche Stunde geht der Eilwagen ab?	At what o'clock does the diligence or stage set off?
Sind Sie auf dem Posthause oder Postamte gewesen?	Have you been to the post-office?
Sind Briefe für mich da?	Are there any letters there for me?

Befehlende Redensarten.   *Imperative Phrases.*

Kommen Sie hierher.	Come here.
Machen Sie die Thüre zu.	Shut the door.
Oeffnen Sie die Thüre.	Open the door.
Machen Sie das Fenster zu.	Shut the window.
Machen Sie das Fenster auf.	Open the window.
Kommen Sie näher.	Come nearer.
Eilen Sie. Mache geschwind.	Make haste.
Lassen Sie uns spazieren gehen.	Let us take a walk.
Spazieren Sie im Garten.	Walk in the garden.
Treten Sie ins Haus.	Go, *or* step into the house.

Gehen Sie aus dem Hause.	Go *or* get out of the house.
Folgen Sie mir nahe.	Follow me close.
Folgen Sie ihm von weitem.	Follow him at a distance.
Sagen Sie ihm, er möge kommen.	Tell him he may come.
Warten Sie einen Augenblick.	Wait a moment.
Gehen Sie hinauf.	Go up.
Kommen Sie herauf.	Come up.
Gehe zu ihm hinauf.	Go up to him.
Komm zu mir herauf.	Come up to me.
Komm die Treppe herauf.	Come up stairs.
Laßt ihn herauf kommen.	Tell him to come up.
Gehen Sie hinunter.	Go down.
Kommen Sie herunter.	Come down.
Komm zu mir herunter.	Come down to me.
Bringen Sie es herunter.	Bring it down.
Belieben Sie sich zu setzen.	Be pleased to sit down.
Stehen Sie auf und gehen.	Get up and walk.
Waschen Sie sich die Hände.	Wash your hands.
Schreiben Sie die Rechnung.	Write the bill, *or* account.
Nehmen Sie das Silber.	Take the silver.
Nehmen Sie es auf.	Take it up.
Zeigen Sie Ihre Handschrift.	Show your writing.
Bestrafen Sie die Faulen.	Punish the idle.
Verlieren Sie nicht alle Hoffnung.	Do not lose all hope.
Dringen Sie durch den Haufen.	Press through the crowd.
Verbessern Sie Ihre Sitten.	Improve your manners.
Verkaufen Sie Ihr Feld.	Sell your field.
Unterschreiben Sie den Contract.	Sign the contract.
Beschließen Sie den Handel.	Conclude the bargain.
Singen Sie ein Lied.	Sing a song.
Putzen Sie das Licht.	Snuff the candle.
Wärme Er mein Bett.	Warm my bed.

Suchen Sie das Feuerzeug.	Look for the fire box.
Gehen Sie zu Bette.	Go to bed.
Verlassen Sie das Bett.	Get out of bed.
Er soll frühe aufstehen.	Let him get up early.
Laß uns geschwind aufstehen.	Let us get up directly.
Geben Sie acht; bleiben Sie.	Take care; stop, *or* wait.
Gehen Sie schnell.	Walk quick.
Sprechen Sie mit ihm.	Speak to him.
Halten Sie es nieder.	Hold it down.
Bleiben Sie ruhig.	Remain quiet.
Halt an, Kutscher!	Stop coachman!
Lassen Sie anspannen.	Order the horses to be put to.
Lassen Sie den Wagen vorfahren.	Bring up the carriage.
Lasse die Pferde beschlagen.	Get the horses shod.
Helfen Sie Ihrer Schwester.	Help your sister.
Fordern Sie Wein.	Ask for some wine.
Füllen Sie die Gläser.	Fill the glasses.
Bring den Senf.	Bring the umstard.
Putzet meine Schuhe.	Clean *or* black my shoes.
Trocknet die Leinwand.	Dry the linen.
Lehren Sie die Schüler.	Teach the scholars.
Erklären Sie die Wörter.	Explain the words.
Erklären Sie die Regeln.	Explain the rules.
Beweisen Sie den Satz.	Prove the proposition.
Verzeihen Sie meinen Fehler.	Excuse my mistake.
Beherrschen Sie Ihre Zunge.	Govern your tongue.
Vermehren Sie Ihre Kenntnisse.	Increase your knowledge.
Achten Sie Ihre Lehrer.	Esteem your teachers.
Verlegen Sie meine Papiere nicht.	Do not displace my papers.
Vernachlässigen Sie Ihre Geschäfte nicht.	Do not neglect your business.
Kommen Sie hierher.	Come this way.

Kommen Sie bald wieder.	Come back soon.
Bleiben Sie da einen Augenblick.	Stay there a moment.
Nehmen Sie gefälligst jenen Weg.	Go *or* take that way, if you please.
Gehen Sie vor Ihren Bruder.	Go before your brother.
Besehen Sie den schönen Wagen.	Look at the beautiful coach.
Trauen Sie ihm nicht.	Do not trust to him.
Trauen Sie meinen Worten.	Take my word for it.
Verlassen Sie sich auf sie.	Rely upon her, *or* them.
Stehen Sie mir bei.	Assist *or* help me.
Schenke den Thee ein.	Pour out the tea.
Mache ihn nicht zu schwach.	Do not make it too weak.
Nehmen Sie Platz.	Take a seat.
Essen Sie. Trinken Sie.	Eat. Drink.
Geben Sie mir ein Glas Wasser.	Give me a glass of water.
Geben Sie mir einen Stuhl.	Give me a chair.
Geben Sie diesem Kinde ein Stück Brod.	Give a bit of bread to that child.
Geben Sie diesem kleinen Mädchen ein Taschentuch.	Give that little girl a pocket-handkerchief.
Legen Sie das Buch auf den Tisch.	Put that book on the table.
Thun Sie, was ich Ihnen sage.	Do what I tell you.
Sage dies nicht; du würdest dir Schaden thun.	Do not say that; you would injure yourself.
Thue es nicht, und du wirst zufrieden seyn.	Do not do it, and you will be pleased.
Höre auf zu weinen.	Give over crying.
Lassen Sie uns aufhören.	Let us have done.
Fangen Sie an. Fahren Sie fort.	Begin. Go on. Continue, *or* proceed.
Hören Sie ihn nicht an.	Do not listen to him.

Von der Zeit.   Of Time.

Ein Jahr. Zwei Jahre.	A year. Two years.
Vor einem Jahre.	A year ago.
Seit einem Jahre.	For a year, *or*, this year.
Seit sechs Monaten.	For, *or* these six months.
Ein halbes Jahr.	Six months.
Seit einem Monat.	For a month past.
Vor einem Monate.	A month ago.
Es ist ein Monat.	It is a month.
Drei Monate her.	Three months ago.
Es sind zwei Monate.	It is two months.
Seit vierzehn Tagen.	For a fortnight past.
Vierzehn Tage her.	A fortnight ago.
Es sind zwei Wochen.	It is two weeks.
Es ist eine Woche.	It is a week.
Es sind drei Tage.	It is three days.
In einem Monate.	In a month.
In drei Monaten.	In three months.
In sechs Wochen.	In six weeks.
In drei Tagen.	In three days.
In einer Stunde.	In an hour.
In Kurzem.	In a short time.
Heute.	To-day.
Diesen Morgen.	This morning.
Mittags.	At noon, *or* mid-day.
Nachmittags.	In the afternoon.
Diesen Nachmittag.	This afternoon.
Diesen Abend.	This evening.
Die künftige Nacht.	The approaching night.
Morgen.	To-morrow.
Uebermorgen.	The day after to-morrow.
Gestern.	Yesterday.
Gestern Abend.	Yesterday evening.

Vorige or vergangene Nacht.	Last night.
Vorgestern.	The day before yesterday.
Alle Tage	Every day.
Dieses Jahr.	This year.
Verflossenes Jahr.	Last year.
Nächstes Jahr.	Next year.
In diesem Monate.	This month.
Verflossenen Monat.	Last month.
Nächsten Monat.	Next month.
Diese Woche.	This week.
Vorige or vergangene Woche.	Last week.
Künftige Woche.	Next week.
Von Zeit zu Zeit.	From time to time.
Nach und nach.	By and by.
Beinahe immer.	Almost always.
Beinahe niemals.	Scarcely, or hardly ever.
Immer. Niemals.	Always. Never.
Früher oder später.	Sooner or later.
Frühestens.	As soon as possible.
Tags, des Tages.	In the day time.
Nachts, des Nachts.	In the night.
Abends, des Abends.	In the evening.
Morgens, des Morgens.	In the morning.
Vormittags, des Vormittags.	In the forenoon.

Nebenwörter, u. s. w. — ADVERBS, &c.

Wo ist mein Bruder?	Where is my brother?
Er ist nicht hier.	He is not here.
Wo gehen Sie hin?	Where are you going?
Ich gehe nach Frankreich.	I am going to France.
Wann werden Sie wieder kommen?	When shall you return?
Ich weiß es nicht, vielleicht niemals.	I do not know, perhaps never.

FAMILIAR PHRASES.

Woher kommen Sie?	Where do you come from?
Ich komme von Leipzig.	I come from Leipsig.
Und wo reisen Sie hin?	And where are you going, *or* travelling to?
Ich gehe nach London.	I am going to London.
Ich gehe weg, ohne zu wissen wohin.	I am going away, without knowing where to.
Warum sind Sie denn hierher gekommen?	Why have you come here then?
Ich weiß es nicht, ich gehe nirgendwo hin.	I do not know, I am going no where.
Sie sind allenthalben.	You are every where.
Gehen Sie anderswo hin?	Go somewhere else.
Sprechen Sie ernsthaft?	Do you speak seriously?
Nein, ich sage es nur scherzweise.	No, I only say it in jest.
Glauben Sie das aufrichtig?	Do you believe that sincerely?
Sie haben es mir schon gesagt.	You have already told me so.
Das kann ich kaum glauben.	That I can hardly believe.

EXAMPLES TO ILLUSTRATE THE NOUNS, &C. OF TIME.

Wie lange sind Sie schon in Deutschland?	How long have you been in Germany?
Ich bin schon vier Monate hier.	I have been here these four months.
Wohnen Sie schon lange in dieser Stadt?	Have you *already* been living long in this town?
Ich bin erst seit einem Monat hier.	I have only been a month here.
Mein Sohn ist vor acht Tagen von Deutschland mit dem Packetbot angekommen.	My son arrived eight days ago from Germany by the packet.

Er ist zehn Jahre in Hamburg gewesen.	He has been ten years in Hamburgh.
Ich habe ihn schon ein ganzes Jahr nicht gesehen.	I have not seen him for a whole year.
Ich bin fünf Monate in diesem Lande.	I have been five months in this country.
Ich bin seit drei Tagen gar nicht aus dem Hause gewesen.	I have not been out of the house for three days, *or* these three days.
Mein Schwager ist Montag vor acht Tagen von hier abgereiset.	My brother-in-law set off from here last Monday sennight, *or* week.
Es war etwa vierzehn Tage her.	It was about a fortnight ago.
Er wird in einer Woche zurückkehren.	He will return in a week.
Lassen Sie uns früh Morgens ausgehen.	Let us go out early in the morning.
Steht ihre Familie gewöhnlich früh des Morgens auf?	Does your family usually rise early in the morning?
Ich bin heute Morgen mit Aufgang der Sonne aufgestanden.	I got up this morning when the sun was rising.

END OF THE FAMILIAR PHRASES.

FOURTH DIVISION.

FAMILIAR DIALOGUES.

Die Begrüßungen.	SALUTATIONS, &c.
Guten Morgen, mein Herr.*	Good morning, Sir.*
Guten Abend, Madame.	Good evening, Ma'am.
Gute Nacht, Mamsell P.	Good night, Miss P.
Wie befinden Sie sich, *or* Wie gehts?	How do you do, Sir, *or* how are you (*vulgar.*)?
Sehr wohl, ich danke Ihnen.	Very well, thank you.
Und wie steht es mit Ihnen?	And how do you do?
Wie ist Ihr Befinden?	How is your health?
Ziemlich wohl, ich danke Ihnen.	Tolerably well, thank you.
Ich hoffe Sie sind wohl.	I hope you are well.
Recht wohl, ich danke.	Quite well, thank you.
Ich freue mich sehr darüber.	I am very glad to hear it.
✗ Ich bin Ihnen sehr verbunden.	I am much obliged to you.
Es ist mir lieb Sie zu sehen.	I am glad to see you.
Ich danke Ihnen herzlich.	I thank you kindly.
Ich bin sehr erfreuet Sie wohl zu sehen.	I am very happy to see you well.
Ich befinde mich sehr wohl, Gott sey Dank.	I am very well, thank God.
Ich hoffe Sie wohl zu sehen.	I hope I see you well.

* *Observe.*—Although it is not the custom in Germany, to address gentlemen by Mein Herr, so frequently as we use *Sir*, in England, yet it would be considered impolite not to address the ladies by Madame or Mamsell.

Ich hoffe Sie bei guter Gesund= | I hope I find you in good
heit anzutreffen. | health.
Ich danke Ihnen, mir ist ganz | I thank you, I am quite
wohl. | well.
So wohl man nur seyn kann. | As well as can be.
Wie haben Sie sich befunden | How have you been since I
seitdem ich Sie zuletzt gesehen | saw you last?
habe?
Nicht sehr wohl. | Not very well.
Ich habe Sie lange nicht gesehen. | I have not seen you for a
 | long time.

Es ist beinahe ein Jahrhundert, | It is almost an age since I
seitdem ich das Vergnügen | had the pleasure of seeing
hatte Sie zu sehen. | you.
Ich habe gerade diesen Morgen | I was just enquiring after
Hrn. H. nach Ihrem Befinden | your health this morning
gefragt. | from Mr. H.
Ich danke Ihnen für Ihre | I thank you for your kind
Aufmerksamkeit. | attention.
Wie steht's mit Ihrem Husten? | How is your cough?
Mein Husten ist seit einiger Zeit | My cough has for some
schlimmer geworden. | time become worse.
Ich höre dies mit Bedauern. | I am very sorry to hear it.
Das ist eine schlimme Nachricht, | That is bad news, I am very
das thut mir sehr leid. | sorry for it.
Doch befinde ich mich heute ein | Yet, I find myself rather
wenig besser. | better to-day.
Dies ist erfreulich, es ist mir | That's well, I am very glad
sehr angenehm es zu hören. | to hear it.
Sie sehen nicht so wohl aus als | You do not look so well as
ich wünschen möchte. | I could wish.
Ich habe mich erkältet, ich habe | I have caught a cold, I have
Ko. | the head-ache.
Sie mi sich warm halten. | You must keep yourself warm.

Ich werde Ihrem freundlichen Rathe folgen, ich will zu Bette gehen.	I shall follow your friendly advice, I will go to bed.
Wie befindet sich Ihre Fräulein Schwester?	How does your sister do? or How is your sister?
Sie ist etwas unpäßlich.	She is rather indisposed.
Das thut mir leid.	I am sorry for it.
Was fehlt ihr?	What ails her?
Sie hat Zahnschmerzen, und einen Husten.	She has the tooth-ache, and has a cough.
Wie lange ist sie krank gewesen?	How long has she been ill?
Nicht sehr lange.	Not very long.
Ich hoffe, die Veränderung des Wetters wird ihr wohl thun.	I hope the change of weather will do her good.
Ich danke Ihnen herzlich.	I thank you kindly.
Empfehlen sie mich ihr bestens.	Present my best respects to her.
Meine besten Wünsche für ihre Wiederherstellung.	My best wishes for her recovery.
Wie befindet sich ihre Frau Gemahlin?	How is your lady?
Seit einigen Tagen befindet sie sich nicht ganz wohl.	She has not been very well for some days.
Doch befindet sie sich heute ein wenig besser.	However, she is rather better to-day.
Dies ist erfreulich. Und wie befinden sich Ihre Kinder?	That's well. And how are your children?
Gott sey Dank, sie genießen alle einer vollkommenen Gesundheit.	Thank God they all enjoy perfect health.
Ich hoffe, alle die Ihrigen sind wohl.	I hope all your family are well.
Ich hoffe, daß Ihr Herr Vater sich wohl befindet.	I hope your father is well.

Ich glaube, er befindet sich wohl; er befand sich gestern Abends wohl.

Und wie befindet sich Ihr Herr Bruder?

Ich danke Ihnen, er befindet sich ziemlich wohl.

Ich hoffe daß Ihre Frau Mutter sich besser befindet.

Ich danke Ihnen, sie ist bei weitem besser.

I believe he is well, he was well last night

And how is your brother?

Thank you, he is tolerably well.

I hope your Mother is better.

Thank you, she is much better.

Vom Essen und Trinken.

OF EATING AND DRINKING.

Geben Sie mir etwas zu essen.
Ich habe guten Appetit.
Mich hungert sehr.
Was wollen Sie essen?
Ich könnte wohl etwas essen.
Ich bin dem Verhungern nahe.
Wir haben nichts als kalten Braten.
Was für Braten?
Kalbsbraten und Schweinebraten.
Das ist alles, was man wünschen kann.
Hätte ich gewußt, daß Sie kommen würden, so würde ich etwas mehr bestellt haben.
Bedienen Sie sich nach Gefallen, ohne Umstände.

Dieses Fleisch ist sehr gut.
Ist Ihnen ein wenig von dem Schweinebraten gefällig?

Give me something to eat.
I have a good appetite.
I am very hungry.
What will you eat?
I could eat something.
I am almost starved.
We have nothing but cold roast meat.
What kind of roast meat?
Roast veal and roast pork.
That is all one can wish.
Had I known that you were coming, I would have ordered something more.
Help yourself to what you like, without any ceremony.

This meat is very good.
Will you take a little of the roast pork?

Ich danke Ihnen, ich habe genug gegessen.
Was trinken Sie gewöhnlich, Halb-Bier oder Porter?
Ich will etwas Halb-Bier trinken.

Das Frühstück.

Ist das Frühstück bereit, or fertig?
Ja, mein Herr, das Frühstück ist fertig.
Um welche Zeit frühstücken Sie gewöhnlich?
Wir frühstücken gewöhnlich um neun Uhr.
Kommen Sie zum Frühstücke, ich bin sehr hungerig.
Setzen Sie sich, or nehmen Sie Platz.
Ich wünsche mein Früstück zu haben.
Bring mir mein Frühstück.
Es stehet alles auf dem Tische.
Kocht das Wasser?
Nein, das Wasser kocht nicht.
Frage die Magd, ob alles fertig ist.
Ist der Caffee gemacht?
Nein, aber der Thee ist gemacht.
Machen Sie ihn nicht zu schwach.
Schenken Sie den Thee ein.
Ist Ihnen Thee, oder Caffee gefällig?

No, thank you, I have eaten enough, or sufficient.
What do you usually drink, table-beer or porter?
I will drink, or take a little table-beer.

BREAKFAST.

Is breakfast ready?
Yes, Sir, breakfast is ready.
At what time do you usually breakfast?
We generally breakfast at nine.
Come to breakfast, I am very hungry.
Sit down, or take a seat.
I want my breakfast, or I want to have my breakfast.
Bring me my breakfast.
Everything is on the table.
Does the water boil?
No, the water does not boil.
Ask the servant whether every thing is ready.
Is the coffee made?
No, but the tea is made.
Do not make it too weak.
Pour out the tea.
Which do you prefer, tea or coffee?

Ich ziehe eine Tasse Thee vor. / I prefer a cup of tea.
Womit soll ich Ihnen aufwarten? / What shall I offer you?
Ich trinke lieber Caffee. / I prefer coffee.
Was wünschen Sie, Madam, Thee oder Coffee? / What will you take Ma'am, tea or coffee?
Beides wenn ich bitten darf. / Both if you please.
Hier ist Zucker, Milch und Rahm. / Here is sugar, milk, and cream.
Bedienen Sie sich nach Ihrem Geschmacke. / Make it to your liking, or help yourself to your liking.

Thun Sie als wenn Sie zu Hause wären. / Do as if you were at home.
Mein Herr A. Sie sind gerate zu rechter Zeit gekommen. / Mr. A. you are just come at the right time.
Sie sollen mit uns frühstücken / You will breakfast with us.
Haben Sie gefrühstückt? / Have you breakfasted?
Noch nicht. / Not yet.
Ist es Zeit zu frühstücken? / Is it time to breakfast?
Ja, es wird gleich heraufgebracht. / Yes, it will be brought up immediately.
Wollen Sie Thee, Caffee, oder Chocolate? / Will you take tea, coffee, or chocolate?
Ich trinke lieber starken Caffee, halb Rahm, und viel Zucker. / I am partial to strong coffee, half cream, and a great deal of sugar.

Ist er süß und stark genug? / Is it sweet and strong enough?

Er ist vortrefflich. / It is excellent.
Wenn er es nicht ist, so bitte ich Sie es zu sagen. / If it be not, I request you will say so.
Wie schmeckt Ihnen der Caffee? / How do you like the coffee?
Ich hoffe, daß er Ihnen schmeckt. / I hope it is to your liking.

Hier ist Brod und Butter, *or* Butterbrod.

Wenn ich zu Hause bin, habe ich gewöhnlich geröstetes Brod.

Ist Ihnen sonst etwas gefällig?

Noch eine Tasse Thee, Herr B.?

Ich danke Ihnen.

Sie haben nur ein leichtes Frühstück genommen.

Wo werden sie den Morgen bis zum Mittagsessen zubringen?

Ich werde ausreiten.

Darf ich Sie bemühen zu klingeln?

Ja wohl.

Johann, nimm die Sachen weg, und räume den Tisch ab.

Vor dem Mittagsessen.

Guten Tag, mein Herr, wie befinden Sie sich?

Sehr wohl, ich danke Ihnen.

Es ist mir lieb Sie wohl zu sehen.

Essen Sie heute Mittag bei uns.

Ich komme, um mit Ihnen zu essen.

Sie sind sehr willkommen.

Sie werden ein einfaches Essen finden.

Wir haben nur unser tägliches Gericht.

Here is bread and butter.

When I am at home, I generally have toast.

Would you like any thing else?

Another cup of tea, Mr. B.?

No, thank you.

You have made a very poor breakfast.

Where shall you pass the morning till dinner time?

I shall take a ride.

May I trouble you to ring the bell?

Yes, to be sure.

John, take away the breakfast things, and clear the table.

BEFORE DINNER.

Good day, Sir, how do you do?

Very well thank you.

I am glad to see you well.

Pray dine with us to-day.

I have come to dine with you.

You are very welcome.

You will find a plain dinner.

We have but our daily fare.

Das ist alles, was man wünschen kann.	That is all that one can wish.
Setzen Sie sich doch. Nehmen Sie Platz.	Pray be seated. Take a seat.
Setzen Sie sich gefälligst neben das Feuer.	Sit down, *or* take a seat near the fire, if you please.
Lassen Sie sich nieder.	Pray sit down.
Ich bin sehr unhöflich, Sie so lange stehen zu lassen.	I am very rude, to let you stand so long.
Sagen Sie das doch nicht.	Do not mention it.
Erlauben Sie, daß ich Ihnen einen Stuhl reiche.	Allow me to hand you a chair.
Bemühen Sie sich nicht.	Do not trouble yourself.
Sie geben sich zu viele Mühe.	You give yourself too much trouble.
Reiche dem Herrn einen Stuhl.	Reach the gentleman a chair.
Um welche Zeit essen wir heute Mittag?	What time do we dine to-day?
Wir werden nicht vor fünf Uhr essen.	We shall not dine before five o'clock.
Warum speisen wir heute so spät?	Why do we dine so late to-day?
Werden wir heute jemand zu Tische haben?	Shall we have any body to dine with us to-day?
Ja wohl, Herrn und Madame R.	Yes, to be sure, Mr. and Mrs. R.
Hast du vergessen, daß wir heute Gesellschaft haben?	Did you not recollect that we have company to-day?
Ich erwarte Herrn B.	I expect Mr. B.
Frau A. hat versprochen zu kommen, wenn das Wetter es erlaubt.	Mrs. A. has promised to come if the weather permit.

Was haben wir zum Mittagsessen?	What have we for dinner?
Was werden wir zum Mittagsessen haben?	What shall we have for dinner?
Wir werden Rinderbraten und Geflügel haben.	We shall have some roast beef and poultry.
Haben Sie das Mittagessen bestellt?	Have you ordered dinner?
Was haben Sie zum Mittagsessen bestellt?	What have you ordered for dinner?
Haben Sie für Fisch ausgeschickt?	Have you sent out for any fish?
Werden wir Fische haben?	Shall we have any fish?
Ich konnte keine bekommen.	I could not get any.
Es war kein Fisch auf dem Markte.	There was no fish in the market.
Ich fürchte, wir werden ein sehr mittelmäßiges Mittagsessen haben.	I fear we shall have a very indifferent dinner.
Wir müssen vorlieb nehmen.	We must do as well as we can.

Das Mittagsessen.   DINNER.

Lassen Sie das Essen auftragen.	Call for dinner, *or* let dinner be brought up.
Es ist noch nicht fertig.	It is not yet ready.
Peter, sage dem Koche, er soll auftragen lassen.	Peter, tell the cook to let dinner be brought up.
Es wird sogleich geschehen.	It will be served up immediately.
Mein Herr, es ist aufgetragen.	Sir, dinner is on the table.
Meine Damen und Herren, ist es Ihnen gefällig in das Speisezimmer zu gehen?	Ladies and gentlemen, will you please to walk into the dining-room?

Meine Herren, nehmen Sie Platz. | Gentlemen. take your seats.
Wollen Sie oben am Tische Platz nehmen, Madame? | Will you take a seat at the upper end of the table Ma'am?
Und Sie, mein Herr P., bei Madame R. | And you Mr. P. by Mrs. R.
Wenn Sie es verlangen, so kann ich nichts dagegen haben. | If you desire it, I can have no objection.
Warum machen Sie so viele Complimente? | Why do you make so much ceremony?
Nehmen Sie Platz hier, Mamsell L., und Sie neben an, mein Herr. | Take a seat here, Miss L., and you next, Sir.
Sind die Gäste alle gekommen? | Is all the company come?
Ja, mein Herr, *or* Madame. | Yes, Sir, *or* Ma'am.
Wer will das Gebet verrichten? | Who says grace?

Bei Tische.

AT TABLE, OR DINNER.

Johann, gieb mir Brod. | John, give me some bread.
Soll ich Ihnen etwas von der oberen oder unteren Rinde geben? | Shall I give you some of the upper or under crust?
Wie es Ihnen beliebt, *or* gleich viel. | As you please, *or* it is all the same.
Womit kann ich Ihnen dienen? | What can I help you to?
Ist Ihnen ein wenig Suppe gefällig? | Will you take a little soup?
Ja, Madame, ich esse sie sehr gerne. | Yes, Ma'am, I like it very much.
Herr M., darf ich Ihnen Suppe anbieten? | Mr. M. shall I offer you some soup?
Ist Ihnen etwas Suppe gefällig? | Will you take some soup?

Wenn es Ihnen gefällig ist.	If you please.
Reichen Sie mir Ihren Teller.	Give me your plate.
Wie schmeckt Ihnen dies?	How do you like it?
Wie finden Sie das?	How do you find it?
In der That, es ist ganz vortrefflich.	It is very excellent indeed.
Ist Ihnen Suppe gefällig, Frau N.?	Will you take a little soup, Mrs N.?
Soll ich Sie bedienen, mein Herr?	Shall I help you, Sir?
Ich danke Ihnen, ich bitte Sie um etwas Lachs.	No, thank you, I will trouble you for some salmon.
Herr P., darf ich Sie bemühen, den Fisch herumzulangen.	Mr. P., may I trouble you to help the fish round.
Nehmen Sie auch Sauce dazu?	Will you take sauce with it?
Hier ist Brühe zum Fisch.	Here is fish sauce.
Haben Sie die Güte, und bedienen sich selbst.	Have the kindness to help yourself.
Dieser Fisch ist vortrefflich, und sehr gut zubereitet.	This fish is excellent, and very well dressed.
Meine Frau ist eine Liebhaberin von allen Arten Fische.	Mrs. R. is partial to all kinds of fish.
Ich habe noch niemand gekannt, der sich wenig aus Fisch gemacht hätte.	I have never known any one who was not fond of fish.
Lieben Sie die Steinbutte?	Do you like turbot, Sir?
Soll ich Ihnen etwas davon geben?	Shall I help you to some?
Ich danke Ihnen. Was für Fisch ist in der Schüssel neben Ihnen?	No, thank you. What fish is that in the dish near you.
Es ist Lachs. Es ist Roche.	It is salmon. It is skate.
Hier ist Kabeljau.	Here is cod-fish.

Ich bitte Sie um etwas, *or* ein wenig Roche.	I will thank you for a small piece of skate.
Hier haben Sie etwas mit der Leber. Die Leber dieses Fisches ist sehr delicat.	Here is some, with some liver. The liver of this fish is very delicate.
Herr N., nehmen Sie selbst Fisch.	Mr. N., help yourself to fish.
Bedienen Sie sich selbst.	Help yourself.
Ist es See- oder Flußfisch?	Is it sea, *or* fresh water fish?
Es sind beide Gattungen hier.	There are both.
Hier ist Hecht, Forelle, Karpfen, und Aal.	Here is pike, trout, carp, and eel.
Was wollen Sie trinken?	What will you drink?
Trinken Sie Bier oder Wein?	Do you drink beer or wine?
Wein, wenn ich bitten darf.	Wine, if you please.
Ich möchte lieber etwas Porter haben.	I should prefer some porter. I should like some porter.
Bitte, geben Sie mir ein Glas Porter.	I will thank you for a glass of porter.
Was sagen Sie von diesem Porter?	What do you think of this porter?
Ist dieses nicht sehr guter Porter?	Is not this very good porter?
Ich kann mich nicht erinnern je besseren getrunken zu haben.	I do not recollect having ever drank better.
Lassen Sie es auf Flaschen zapfen?	Do you bottle it?
Wie lange ist es abgezapft gewesen?	How long has it been in bottle?
Sechs oder sieben Monate.	Six or seven months.
Wollen Sie Kartoffeln? Sind Ihnen Kartoffeln gefällig?	Will you take some potatoes?
Wenn ich bitten darf.	If you please.
Wollen Sie ein Glas Wein mit mir trinken?	Will you take a glass of wine with me?

Herzlich gerne. Mit vielem Vergnügen.	Willingly. With much pleasure.
Ist Ihnen rother oder weißer gefällig?	Will you take white or red?
Ich werde etwas weißen trinken, wenn Sie erlauben.	I will take some white, if you please.
Bringe zwei Gläser Wein, eins roth, und eines weiß.	Bring two glasses of wine, one of red and one of white.
Herr N., Ihre Gesundheit.	Your health, Sir.
Ich habe die Ehre Ihre Gesundheit zu trinken.	I have the honor to drink your health.
Dieser Wein ist sehr gut.	This wine is very good.
Herr L., kosten Sie doch diesen Wein, er ist vortrefflich, es ist alter Hochheimer.	Mr. L. do taste this wine, it is excellent, it is old Hochheimer *or* Hock.
Noch ein Glas, Herr L.	Another glass Mr. L.
Es ist alter Hochheimer Rheinwein, er ist länger als fünf Jahre in meinem Keller.	It is old hock, I have had it more than five years in my cellar.
Es gibt wenige Häuser, wo man ihn so gut trifft.	There are few houses where you can get it so good.
Ich habe immer einen wohlgefüllten Keller geliebt.	I have always liked to have a cellar well stocked.
Kosten Sie diesen Champagner, er ist nicht übel.	Taste this Champagne, it is not bad.
Er ist vortrefflich, ich habe lange keinen solchen guten getrunken.	It is excellent, I have not drank any so good for a long time.
Ich werde Sie um ein wenig Rindfleisch bitten, es sieht so schön aus.	I will thank you for a little beef, it looks so very nice.
Von welcher Seite soll ich es schneiden?	On which side shall I cut it?

Von welcher Sie wollen.

Welchen Theil haben Sie am liebsten?
Essen Sie gerne was gar ist oder nicht?
Was gar ist, wenn ich bitten darf.
Was nicht gar ist.
Darf ich Sie um noch ein Stückchen Rindfleisch bitten?
Ich esse es gerne gar.
Ich esse es gerne nicht zu gar.
Habe ich Ihnen gegeben, was Sie gerne essen?
Ja ich ziehe das vor, was nicht zu gar ist.
Habe ich Ihnen gegeben, was Sie am liebsten essen?
Ich hoffe, daß dieses Stück nach Ihrem Geschmack ist.
Es ist sehr gut.
Darf ich Sie um (*or* für) den Senf bitten?
Herr P., ist Ihnen etwas von dem Rinderbraten gefällig?
Soll ich Ihnen etwas von den Lendenbraten vorlegen?
Wenn ich bitten darf, aber vergessen Sie sich selbst auch nicht.
Essen Sie das Braune gerne?
Ist Ihnen das Braune gefällig?

Either *or* on which you like.
Which part do you prefer, *or* like best?
Do you like it well done, or underdone?
Well done, if you please.

Underdone.
May I trouble you for another slice of beef?
I like it well done.
I do not like it over done.
Have I helped you to what you like?

Yes, I prefer it rather underdone.
Have I helped you to the part you like best?

I hope this piece is to your liking.
It is very good.
May I trouble you for the mustard.
Mr. P., will you take some roast beef?
Shall I help you to a bit of the sirloin?
If you please, but do not forget yourself.

Do you like the outside, *or* are you fond of the outside?

Essen Sie gerne fettes Fleisch?	Do you like fat meat?
Ist Ihnen etwas von dem Fetten gefällig?	Do you choose any fat?
Ich esse das Fette eben nicht sehr gern.	I am not very fond of fat.
Ziehen Sie das Fette oder das Magere vor?	Do you prefer the fat or the lean?
Ein wenig von beiden.	A little of both.
Geben Sie mir etwas von dem Mageren, wenn ich bitten darf.	Give me some of the lean, if you please,
Hier ist ein Stück, welches Sie hoffentlich gern essen werden.	Here is a piece which I hope you will like.
Wie schmeckt Ihnen der Rinderbraten?	How do you like the roast beef?
Er ist in der That sehr gut, ich esse ein gutes Stück Rinderbraten gerne.	It is very good indeed, I am partial to a good piece of roast beef.
Es ist mir sehr lieb, daß er nach ihrem Geschmacke ist.	I am very glad it is to your taste, *or* liking.
Sie haben keine Brühe.	You have no gravy.
Ich habe völlig genug, ich danke Ihnen.	I have quite sufficient, I thank you.
Johann, nimm dieses alles weg, und trage das zweite Gericht auf.	John, take away all these things and bring the second course.
Meine Herren, die Schüsseln stehen vor Ihnen, bedienen Sie sich.	Gentlemen, you have dishes by you, help yourselves.
Nehmen Sie, ohne Complimente, was Ihnen am besten gefällt.	Take, without ceremony, what you like best.
Gib mir einen andren Teller.	Change my plate.
Einen reinen Teller.	A clean plate.

Ein Messer und eine Gabel.	A knife and fork.
Einen Löffel, wenn ich bitten darf.	A spoon, if you please.
Eine Gabel mit drei Zinken.	A three pronged fork.
Bringe dies zur Frau S.	Take this to Mrs. S.
Dieses ist für Fräulein S.	This is for Miss S.
Mein Herr S., was soll ich Ihnen schicken?	Mr. S. what shall I send you?
Erlauben Sie mir, erst die Hühner, welche vor mir stehen, zu zerlegen und herumzugeben.	Permit me first to carve the fowls which stand by me, and to help others.
Was ist Ihnen gefällig, ein Flügel oder die Brust?	Which do you like best, a wing or the breast?
Sie müssen es mir verzeihen, wenn ich einen Schenkel vorziehe.	You must pardon me for preferring a leg.
Ich weiß, gemeiniglich wird eben nicht viel daraus gemacht.	I know that in general it is not much thought of.
Erlauben Sie, daß ich das Geflügel vorschneide.	Permit me to cut up the fowls.
Ich bitte um einen Flügel.	I shall be obliged to you for a wing.
Wollen Sie auch Brühe dazu?	Do you take sauce with it?
Wenn ich Sie bemühen darf.	If I may trouble you.
Soll ich Ihnen etwas Gemüse vorlegen?	Shall I help you to some vegetables?
Hier ist Spinat und Brocoli.	Here is spinage and brocoli.
Schmeckt es Ihnen?	Is it to your liking?
Ich esse alles Geflügel, als Hühnchen, Gänse, Enten, und Truthähne, sehr gerne.	All kinds of poultry, chickens, geese, ducks, and turkeys, are agreeable eating to me.

Laſſen Sie mich den Schinken anſchneiten, er iſt ſehr gut.

Erlauben Sie, daß ich Ihnen etwas Entenbraten vorlege.

Was eſſen Sie für Gemüſe?

Wollen Sie Erbſen, Kartoffeln, oder Blumenkohl?

Da ſind Erbſen, und hier ſind Spargel.

Verſuchen Sie dieſen Kohl, ich denke, er wird Ihnen ſchmecken.

Iſt Ihnen Weißbrot, oder Schwarzbrot gefällig?

Es iſt mir einerlei.

Soll ich Ihnen ein Bißchen von dieſem vorlegen?

Geben Sie mir ſehr wenig.

Soll ich Ihnen ein Stückchen von dieſer Hammelkeule ſchicken?

Sie ſcheint vortrefflich zu ſeyn, ſie iſt ſehr ſaftig.

Ich habe keinen Appetit mehr, ich habe genug gegeſſen.

Dieſer Herr bittet ſich noch ein wenig Schinken aus.

Soll ich Ihnen von den Rebhühnern oder von den Faſanen vorlegen?

Was Ihnen beliebt.

Was eſſen Sie am liebſten, einen Flügel oder einen Schenkel?

Let me carve the ham, it is a very fine one.

Give me leave to help you to some roast duck.

What vegetables do you eat?

Will you have peas, potatoes, or cauliflowers?

There are some peas, and here is asparagus.

Try this cabbage, I think it will please, you, *or* will be to your taste.

Will you have white or brown bread?

It is indifferent to me.

Shall I help you to a bit of this?

Give me very little.

Shall I send you a small piece of this leg of mutton?

It appears to be excellent, it is full of gravy.

I have no longer any appetite, I have eaten enough.

This gentleman will trouble you again for some ham.

Shall I help you to some partridge, or some pheasant?

Which you please.

Which do you like best, a wing or a leg?

Das ist mir gleich, aber Sie bedienen alle, und Sie selbst essen nicht.	I have no choice, but you are carving for all, and eat nothing yourself.
Sie haben keinen Pudding gehabt.	You have had no pudding.
Diese Fricandelle ist köstlich.	This fricandeau is delicious.
Soll ich Ihnen etwas davon vorlegen?	Shall I help you to some of it?
Ich bitte um ein sehr kleines Stück, um es doch zu versuchen.	I will thank you for a very small piece just to taste it.
Geben Sie mir sehr wenig.	Give me very little.
Sie sind ein schlechter Esser, Sie essen nichts.	You are a poor eater, you eat nothing.
Ich bitte um Verzeihung, ich esse sehr viel.	I beg your pardon, I eat very well, *or* very heartily.
Nun, was soll ich Ihnen anbieten?	Now, what shall I offer you?
Ich danke Ihnen, nichts mehr.	Not any thing more, I thank you.
Der Kalbsbraten ist sehr mürbe, *or* weich.	The roast veal is very tender.
Ich muß wirklich um Entschuldigung bitten.	I must indeed beg to be excused.
Ich will Ihnen nur ein kleines Stückchen geben.	I will only give you a small piece.
Sie sind überaus gütig, Sie wollen es sich nicht abschlagen lassen.	You are extremely obliging, you will not be refused.
Geben Sie mir denn ein sehr kleines Stückchen.	Give me then a very small piece.
Es freuet mich, daß Sie sich besonnen haben.	I am glad you have changed your mind.

Ich kann nicht umhin, es sieht so köstlich aus.	I cannot do otherwise, it looks so nice.
Ich will Ihnen ein Bißchen von diesem jungen Huhne schicken.	I will send you a small piece, or a bit of this fowl.
Ein kleines Stückchen von dem jungen Huhne kann Ihnen nicht schaten.	A small piece of the fowl cannot hurt you.
Bringe einen Teller für ten Herrn.	Bring a plate for this gentleman?
Erlauben Sie, daß ich Sie noch einmal bediene?	Permit me to help you again.
Nichts mehr, ich muß aufhören.	Nothing more, I must leave off.
Sie haben mir zu viel gegeben.	You have given me too much.
Ich habe völlig genug.	I have quite sufficient.
Geben Sie mir nur die Hälfte von dem.	Give me only half of that.
Schneiden Sie es halb durch.	Cut that in two.
Ist das genug?	Is that enough?
Das ist ganz genug, ich danke Ihnen.	That is quite sufficient, thank you.
Sie essen wahrlich sehr wenig.	You eat very little indeed.
Ich denke, Sie haben sehr wenig gegessen.	I think you have eaten very little.
Ich bitte um Verzeihung, ich habe eine sehr gute Mahlzeit gemacht.	I beg your pardon, I have made a very good dinner.
Wir haben noch keine Torte, Eierrahm, oder Gallerte gehabt.	We have not yet had any tart, custard, or jelly.
O, sprechen Sie nicht von mehr Leckerbissen, wir haben genug gegessen.	O, do not speak of any more luxuries, we have dined so well.

K

Sie werden ein Stückchen Apfel= torte essen.	You will eat a bit of apple tart.
Ich danke Ihnen, nichts mehr.	I thank you, nothing more.
Ich bin der Letzte am Tische.	I am the last at the table.
Verzeihen Sie mir, Sie haben vorgeschnitten, und ich auch, deswegen sind wir die Letzten.	Pardon me, you have been carving, and I too; on that account we are last.
Ich glaube, Sie essen bloß um mich nicht zu beschämen.	I believe you are eating merely to keep me in countenance.
Sir irren sich in der That; ich bin noch nicht fertig, ich werde ein wenig Käse essen.	You are mistaken, I have not yet done, I shall eat a bit of cheese.
Ihr könnt jetzt wegnehmen.	You may now take away.
Nimm ab, und bringe den Wein.	Take away, and bring the wine.

Der Nachtisch.   THE DESSERT.

Johann, trage den Wein und das Obst auf.	John, put the wine and fruit on the table.
Erlauben Sie mir Ihnen etwas Obst zu schicken.	Allow me to send you some fruit.
Hier sind Pfirsiche, Abricosen, Nectarinen, Birnen, Aepfel, Trauben und Stachelbeeren.	Here are peaches, apricots, nectarines, pears, apples, grapes, and gooseberries.
Wir hätten Kirschen, Johan= nisbeeren, Erdbeeren, und Melonen haben sollen; sie waren aber leider nicht mehr zu bekommen.	We should have had cherries, currants, strawberries, and melons; but unfortunately they were not to be had.
Da sind Nüsse, Mandeln und Rosinen, Oliven, Apfelsinen und Feigen.	There are nuts, almonds and raisins, olives, oranges, and figs.

Ich werde eine Weintraube essen.	I will eat a bunch of grapes.
Wählen Sie was Sie gern essen.	Choose what you like, or take what you please.
Da haben Sie Pflaumen, Kastanien und Haselnüsse.	There are plums, chesnuts, and filberts.
Wo kaufen Sie diese schönen Früchte?	Where do you buy these fine fruits?
Hier in der Stadt, sie sind aber sehr selten.	Here in town, but they are very scarce.
Darf ich Ihnen ein Glas von diesem Weine anbieten?	May I offer you a glass of this wine?
Hier sind Port, Xeres, Madeira, Champagner, und rother Franzwein.	Here are Port, Sherry, Madeira, Champagne, and Claret.
Welcher ist Ihnen gefällig?	Which will you please to have?
Ich ziehe ein Glas Portwein vor.	I prefer a glass of port.
Ich hoffe, Sie werden ihn gut finden.	I hope you will find it good.
Mein Herr H., haben Sie diese ganze Zeit etwas getrunken?	Mr. H. have you drank any thing all this time?
Nein, ich bin mit Essen beschäftigt gewesen.	No, Sir, I have been occupied with eating.
Wollen Sie nicht ein Glas Wein trinken?	Will you not drink a glass of wine?
Soll ich Ihnen noch ein Glas hiervon, oder von einem andern einschenken?	Shall I pour you out a glass of the same, or of any other?
Hiervon, wenn Sie die Güte haben wollen.	Of the same, if you please, or will have the goodness.
Dieser Wein ist vortrefflich.	This wine is excellent.
Bekommen Sie ihn von einem Weinhändler?	Do you get it from a wine-merchant?

Nein, ich bekomme ihn aus der ersten Hand.

Es giebt wenige Häuser, wo man ihn so gut bekommen kann.

Ich bekomme ihn Faßweise.

Ich kaufe ihn von einem Weinhändler, der ihn von dem Hause der Herren Ruskin, Telford und Domecq hat.

Ich habe gehört, daß die Weine, welche sie einführen, von der ersten Güte sind.

Ja, Sie haben recht, es ist ganz wahr.

Vor kurzem wurde ein einziges Faß von ihrem Xereswein für sechs hundert Pfund Sterling verkauft.

Das muß ein Wein von einer vortrefflichen Qualität gewesen seyn.

Ihr Portwein hat viel Kraft, und eine angenehme Herbe, welche ich lieber mag als dünne Weine.

Hierin ist unser Geschmack verschieden; ich ziehe immer Champagner und Burgunder vor, aber noch mehr alten Rheinwein.

Kosten Sie diesen Champagner.

Ich habe die Ehre Ihre Gesundheit zu trinken.

No, I get it at the first hand.

There are few houses where one can get it so good.

I have it by the butt.

I buy it of a wine merchant who has it from the firm of Messrs. Ruskin, Telford and Domecq.

I have heard that the wines they import are of the best quality.

Yes, you are right, it is quite true.

A short time ago, a single butt of their sherry was sold for six hundred pounds.

That must have been a wine of very superior quality.

Your port wine has a good body, and has an agreeable roughness, which I like better than thin wines.

There we differ in taste, I am always partial to Champagne and Burgundy, but still more to old Hock.

Taste this Champagne.

I have the honour to drink your health.

Ich danke Ihnen *or* ich bin Ihnen sehr verbunden.

Auf die Gesundheit Ihrer ganzen Familie, und auf die Ihrer Freunde.

Mein Herr, Sie erzeigen mir eine Ehre.

Thank you, *or* I am very much obliged to you.

To the health of all your family, and that of your friends.

Sir, you do me honor.

Beim Theetrinken.

ON DRINKING TEA.

Der Thee ist fertig; wollen Sie sich in die andere Stube begeben?

Habet ihr das Theezeug hineingetragen?

Es ist alles auf dem Tische.

Ich will Ihnen den Kessel bringen.

Der Thee ist ganz fertig.

Die Gesellschaft wartet auf Sie.

Ich komme, ich folge Ihnen.

Wir haben nicht Tassen genug.

Uns fehlen noch zwei Obertassen und eine Untertasse.

Du hast die Zuckerzange nicht gebracht.

Bringe noch einen Löffel, und vergiß nicht uns Messer zu bringen.

Ist Ihnen Zucker und Rahm gefällig?

Wie finden Sie diesen Thee?

Er ist Ihnen vielleicht nicht stark genug.

Tea is ready; will you retire, *or* go into the other room?

Have you carried in the tea-things?

Every thing is on the table.

I will bring you the kettle.

Tea is quite ready.

The company are waiting for you.

I am coming, I will follow you.

We have not cups enough.

We want two more cups and a saucer.

You have not brought the sugar tongs.

Bring another spoon, and do not forget to bring us some knives.

Do you take sugar and cream?

How do you find this tea?

It is perhaps not strong enough for you.

Er ist vortrefflich; aber ein wenig zu stark für mich.
It is excellent, but it is a little too strong for me.

Dürfte ich Sie wohl um ein wenig mehr Milch bitten?
May, *or* might I trouble you for a little more milk?

Ich mag ihn nicht so stark, und werde ein wenig heißes Wasser dazu gießen.
I do not like it so strong, and will pour a little hot water to it.

Was ist Ihnen gefällig? Hier sind Kuchen und Semmel.
What will you take? Here are cakes and muffins.

Ich will ein Stückchen Butterbrot nehmen.
I will take a bit of bread and butter.

Bringe noch mehr Butterbrot.
Get some more bread and butter.

Dieser Thee ist sehr gut. Wo haben Sie ihn gekauft?
This tea is very good. Where did you buy it?

Ich habe ihn in London bei Herrn M. in der F. Straße gekauft.
I bought it in London, at Mr. M's., in F. street.

Ich bitte um noch eine Tasse Thee.
I will thank you for another cup of tea.

Mit Vergnügen; nehmen Sie geröstetes Brod; die Butter ist frisch und vortrefflich.
With pleasure; take some toast, the butter is excellent and fresh.

Kellner, *or* Marqueur,* bring uns frische Eier.
Waiter, bring us some fresh eggs.

Wollen Sie nicht noch eine Tasse trinken?
Will you not drink another cup?

Nicht mehr, ich danke Ihnen.
No more, thank you.

Ich will Ihnen noch eine halbe Tasse einschenken.
I will pour you out half a cup.

Ich habe drei Tassen gehabt, und mehr trinke ich nie.
I have had three cups, and I never drink more.

Gewiß nicht?
Are you quite sure?

* *Observe.*—The French word *Marqueur* is used instead of Kellner, in the North-west part of Germany.

Ganz gewiß, ich danke Ihnen.	Quite certain, thank you.
Ich fürchte, Sie mögen ihn nicht.	I am afraid you do not like it.
Wirklich, er schmeckt mir recht gut.	Indeed I do, it is very good.

Das Abendessen.   SUPPER.

Erlauben Sie mir Frau S., Ihnen jetzt guten Abend zu wünschen.	Permit me now, Ma'am, to wish you a good evening.
Warum denn so eilig?	Why in such a hurry?
Bleiben Sie doch zum Abendessen bei uns.	Stay and take supper with us.
Um wie viel Uhr essen Sie?	At what time, *or* hour do you sup?
Um drei Viertel auf neun.	At a quarter before nine.
Wir essen gerade um zehn Uhr.	We sup precisely at ten.
Meine Herren, das Abendessen ist aufgetragen.	Gentlemen, supper is *ready*, (*brought up.*)
Laßt uns schnell gehen, da es schon spät ist.	Let us be quick, as it is late already.
Sollen wir uns niedersetzen?	Shall we be seated?
Wenn es Ihnen beliebt.	If you please.
Meine Damen und Herren, nehmen Sie Platz.	Ladies and gentlemen, take your seats, *or* be seated.
Wir haben nur ein häusliches Abendessen; wir behandeln Sie nicht wie Fremde.	We have only a plain supper; we make no strangers of you.
Ich esse gewöhnlich nichts anders als Brod und Käse.	I usually eat nothing but bread and cheese.
Ich gebe Ihnen bloß Sandwiches.	I only give you sandwiches.
Das ist ein sehr gutes Abendessen.	That is a very good supper.

Wir haben sehr oft ein warmes Abendessen.	We have very often a warm supper.
Es war nichts in der Stadt zu bekommen.	There was nothing to be had in the town.
Es ist zuweilen wirklich sehr unangenehm.	It is sometimes, indeed, very disagreeable.
Ihre häusliche Lebensweise ist sehr gut.	Your plain fare is very good.
Es fehlt uns an Tellern.	We want more plates.
Herr N., wollen Sie wohl diesen Teller weiter geben?	Mr. N., will you be so kind as to hand this plate?
Wollen Sie wohl die Güte haben, und mir das Salzfaß geben?	Will you have the goodness to give me the salt-cellar?
Wollen Sie nicht ein Glas Bier trinken?	Will you not take a glass of beer?
Erlauben Sie mir Ihnen ein Glas einzuschenken.	Allow me to pour you out a glass.
Darf ich Ihnen von diesem Endivien-Salat vorlegen?	Shall I help you to some of this endive?
Nein, ich bin Ihnen sehr verbunden; ich werde ein Hammelsrippchen, *or* eine Hammelscotelette essen.	No, thank you, I will eat a mutton chop.
Ich bin der Meinung, daß vieles Essen des Abends gar nicht gesund ist.	I have an idea that much food at night is not healthy *or* wholesome.
Ich bin ganz anderer Meinung, und ich bemerke, daß die Thiere es auch sind; sie schlafen beständig mit vollem Magen.	I am quite of a different opinion; and I observe that animals are the same, they always sleep on a full stomach.

Der Abend.

Wo wollen Sie diesen Abend hingehen?

Ich kann es kaum sagen.

Wollen Sie mit mir ins Schauspiel gehen?

Ich habe Lust hinzugehen.

Was für ein Stück wird gegeben?

Ist es ein Trauerspiel oder ein Lustspiel, ein Schauspiel oder eine komische Oper?

Es ist ein neues Stück, und heißt „der Fremde."

Sind die Schauspieler gut?

Wer wird den Fremden spielen?

Ohne Zweifel wird Herr K. den Fremden spielen.

Haben Sie den Zettel nicht gelesen?

Haben Sie Billette?

Haben Sie eine Loge?

Das Haus wird heute gedrängt voll werden.

Wir müssen gleich gehen, sonst kommen wir zu spät.

Von Herzen gern; wir wollen keinen Augenblick versäumen, ich bin ganz fertig.

Es ist wie ich befürchtete; das Haus ist jetzt so voll, daß kein guter Platz mehr für uns übrig bleibt.

THE EVENING.

Where will you go this evening?

I can scarcely say.

Will you go with me to the play?

I have a good mind to go.

What play will be performed?

Is it a tragedy or comedy, a drama, or a comic opera?

It is a new piece called "The Stranger."

Are the performers good?

Who is to perform the Stranger?

Without doubt, Mr. K. will perform the Stranger.

Have you not read the bill?

Have you any tickets?

Have you a Box?

The house will be crowded to night.

We must go immediately, otherwise we shall be too late.

With all my heart, we will not lose a moment, I am quite ready.

It is as I feared; the house is now so full, that no good place remains for us.

Wir müssen suchen.
Was werden Sie diesen Abend thun?
Wollen Sie ins Concert gehen?
Nein, mein Herr, lassen Sie uns früh Abendbrod essen, und nach Vauxhall gehen.
Recht gerne; wir werden dort vortreffliche Musick hören.

Lieben Sie Musik?
Ja, ich liebe sie sehr.
Ist das Orchester gut?
Ja, Madame, es ist sehr gut.

Da wir beschlossen haben, nach Vauxhall zu gehen, so müssen wir bestimmen, wie wir hingehen wollen.
Wollen Sie zu Wasser gehen?
Ich mag nicht gern über die Themse fahren.
Lassen Sie uns lieber eine Miethkutsche nehmen.
Wie es Ihnen gefällig ist, mir ist es gleich.
Wie gefällt Ihnen diese Musik?

Mir dünkt, sie ist sehr schön.
Madame Grisi hat eine schöne und natürliche Stimme, es ist nichts Geziertes darin.
Was denken Sie von Vauxhall?

We must look about.
What shall you do with yourself this evening?
Will you go to the concert?
No, Sir, let us sup early, and go to Vauxhall.
With all my heart, (or willingly), we shall hear excellent music.

Do you like music?
Yes, I like it very much.
Is the orchestra good?
Yes, Ma'am, it is very good.

Since we have determined on going to Vauxhall, we must agree how we shall go *there*.
Will you go by water?
I do not like crossing, or to cross the Thames.
Let us rather take a coach. (a hackney-coach.)
As you please, it is all the same to me.
How do you like this music?

I think it is very fine.
Madam Grisi has a fine and natural voice, there is nothing affected in it.
What do you think of Vauxhall?

Es gibt nichts Prächtigeres, es ist ein irdisches Paradies.

Die große Anzahl Lampen, und ihre verschiedenen Farben machen einen so schönen Anblick als man nur sehen kann.

There is nothing more magnificent, it is an earthly Paradise.

The great number of lamps, and their various colors, produce as fine a sight as one can see.

Vom Wetter.

Wie ist das Wetter? *or* Was für Wetter ist es?
Was ist es für Wetter?
Es ist sehr schönes Wetter.
Es ist schlechtes Wetter?
Regnet es?
Ja, mein Herr, es regnet, es regnet sehr stark.
Es hat die ganze Nacht geregnet.
Das Wetter ist jetzt sehr trübe.

Ich glaube, daß wir Regen bekommen werden.
Der Himmel ist bedeckt, wolkig.
Wir werden Gewitter bekommen.
Das Wetter hat sich geändert.
Ich fürchte, wir werden Regen bekommen.
Es rieselt, es wird regnen.
Es fängt an zu regnen.
Ich glaube, es ist nur ein Schauer, es wird bald vorübergehen.
Es ist unbeständiges und veränderliches Wetter.

OF THE WEATHER.

How is the weather?

What sort of weather is it?
It is very fine weather.
It is bad weather.
Does it rain?
Yes, Sir, it rains, it pours, *or* it rains very fast.
It has rained all night.
The weather is now very dull.

I think we shall have rain.

The sky is cloudy.
We shall have a storm.
The weather has changed.
I fear we shall have rain.

It drizzles, it will rain.
It is beginning to rain.
I think it is only a shower, it will soon be over.

It is unsettled and changeable weather.

Ich glaube nicht, daß es diesen Morgen regnen wird; das Wetter klärt sich auf.	I do not think it will rain this morning; the weather is clearing up.
Es ist sehr windig, der Wind wehet sehr stark.	It is very windy; the wind blows very hard.
Wir haben einen heftigen Sturm, sowohl auf dem Lande als zur See gehabt.	We have had a violent storm, both by land and sea.
Wir haben einen sehr starken Wind gehabt.	We have had a very strong wind.
Der Wind ist sehr heftig.	The wind is very violent.
Es weht ein starker Wind.	There is a great deal of wind.
Wir hatten gestern einen heftigen Sturm.	We had yesterday a great storm.
Man merkt, daß der Wind sich gedrehet hat.	One perceives that the wind has changed.
Woher kommt der Wind?	From what quarter does the wind come?
Seit drei Wochen haben wir Westwind.	We have had a west wind for three weeks.
Es ist wahrscheinlich, daß er von derselben Seite anhalten wird.	It is probable it will continue in the same quarter.
In der vorigen Woche haben wir Ostwind gehabt.	Last week we had an east-wind.
Die Luft wird jetzt viel gelinder.	The air now becomes much milder.
Wir werden einen gelinden Wind aus Süden bekommen.	We shall have a mild wind from the south.
Was weht jetzt für ein Wind?	What wind blows now?
Der Wind kommt aus Norden oder Nordost.	The wind comes from the North, or North-east.
Hören Sie den Wind brausen?	Do you hear the wind roaring?

Ja, wie er durch die Bäume pfeift.	Yes, how it whistles through the trees.
Die Luft ist jetzt viel kühler geworden.	The air is now become much cooler.
Wie ist das Wetter heute?	How is the weather to-day?
Es scheint mir, *or* mir scheint es außerordentlich warm.	I think it is, *or* it appears exceedingly warm.
Die Hitze ist sehr beschwerlich.	The heat is very oppressive.
Das Wetter ist den ganzen Tag schön gewesen.	The weather has been fine the whole day.
Es ist nicht zu warm und nicht zu kalt.	It is neither too warm nor too cold.
Dieses Wetter ist kaum auszuhalten, doch es ist der Jahreszeit angemessen.	This weather is scarcely bearable, yet it is seasonable weather.
Im Sommer hat man nichts anders zu erwarten.	In summer we have nothing else to expect.
Die schwühle Hitze macht mich matt.	Sultry weather makes me faint.
Ich mag nicht gerne solches Wetter.	I do not like such weather.
Wenn der Tag heiß ist, so wird es gewöhnlich des Abends schwühl.	When the day is hot, it usually becomes sultry in the evening.
Was werden wir jetzt für Wetter bekommen?	What weather shall we have now?
Ich glaube, wir werden diesen Abend ein Gewitter bekommen, es ist den ganzen Tag sehr heiß gewesen.	I think we shall have thunder this evening; it has been very hot all the day.
Die brennend heißen Tage werden bald kommen.	The burning hot days will soon come.

Ueber die deutsche Sprache.

ON THE GERMAN LANGUAGE.

Sprechen Sie deutsch?	Do you speak German?
Ich lerne es, ich spreche erst ein wenig.	I am learning it, I speak it but little.
Ich verstehe es besser, als ich es sprechen kann.	I understand it better than I can speak it.
Lassen Sie uns deutsch sprechen.	Let us speak German.
Das ist ein gutes Mittel es zu lernen.	That is a good way to learn it.
Ich fange es erst eben an.	I am only just beginning.
Sie werden es bald lernen.	You will soon learn it.
Ich habe die Bemerkung gemacht, daß die Engländer in sehr kurzer Zeit die deutsche Sprache lernen.	I have observed that the English learn the German language in a very short time.
Was denken Sie von der deutschen Sprache?	What do you think of the German language?
Ich denke, sie ist eine sehr nützliche Sprache.	I think it is a very useful language.
Ich denke, sie ist sehr schwer, sie ist sehr wortreich.	I think it is very difficult; it is very copious.
Wie lange haben Sie deutsch gelernt?	How long have you learnt German?
Ich habe es sechs Monate gelernt.	I have learnt it six months.
Das ist nur eine kurze Zeit; ich wundere mich, daß Sie schon so gut sprechen.	That is but a short time; I wonder you speak so well already.
Sie sprechen sehr gut deutsch.	You speak German very well.
Sie schmeicheln mir.	You are flattering me.
Sind Sie in Deutschland gewesen?	Have you been in Germany?

Nein, niemals, ich habe die deutsche Sprache in London und Paris gelernt.	No, never, I have learnt the German language in London and Paris.
Verstehen Sie was Sie lesen?	Do you understand what you read?
Ich lese es besser als ich es spreche.	I read it better than I speak it.
Lernen Sie nicht die Zeitwörter?	Do you not learn the verbs?
Ich habe die Declination der Nennwörter gelernt.	I have learnt the declension of nouns.
Welcher Sprachlehre bedienen Sie sich?	What grammar do you make use of?
Der von Herrn Rowbotham.	Of that of Mr. Rowbotham.
Uebersetzen Sie die deutsche Sprache?	Do you translate German?
Ja, ich übersetze Fabeln aus dem Deutschen ins Englische.	Yes, I translate fables from German into English.
Das ist sehr gut zum Anfange.	That is very well at the beginning.
Habe ich richtig ausgesprochen?	Did I pronounce correctly?
Sprechen Sie zu mir?	Do you speak to me?
Sprechen Sie ein wenig lauter.	Speak a little louder.

Vom Briefschreiben.

OF LETTER WRITING, &c.

Ich möchte gern einen Brief schreiben.	I want to write a letter.
Bringen Sie mir Papier, Federn und Siegellack.	Bring me some paper, pens, and sealing-wax.
Ich habe kein Tintenfaß; darf ich mich des Ihrigen bedienen?	I have no inkstand; may I use yours?
Nehmen Sie es, und brauchen Sie es so lange Sie wollen.	Take it, Sir, and use it as long as you like.
Ist ein Papierhändler in der Nähe?	Is there a stationer in the neighbourhood?

Es wohnt einer in dieser Straße; der dritte oder vierte Laden rechts, wenn Sie aus der Thüre treten.

Ich brauche nur ein wenig Tinte; diese Tinte ist zu blaß, sie taugt nichts.

Kellner, or Marqueur, gehe und kaufe, was der Herr nöthig hat.

Ja, ich danke Ihnen, hier ist Geld; kaufen Sie mir auch ein Buch Fließpapier.

Lassen Sie mir diese Federn verbessern.

Wie haben Sie sie gern? Wollen Sie die Spitze fein oder grob geschnitten haben?

Weder zu fein noch zu grob.

Wenn diese Feder nicht gut ist, so nehmen Sie jene, und hier ist das Federmesser, schneiden Sie sie selbst nach Ihrer Hand.

Geben Sie mir ein Federmesser; ich will meine Feder schneiden.

Dieses Federmesser taugt nichts.

Ich habe kein Petschaft; holen Sie mir eins; hier ist meines.

Wo ist das Tintenfaß?

Wollen Sie mir das Ihrige leihen?

There is one in this street; the third of fourth shop on the right, on going out of the door.

I only want a little ink; this ink is too pale, it is good for nothing.

Waiter, go and buy what the gentleman wants.

Yes, I'll thank you, here is some money; buy me also a quire of blotting-paper.

Get these pens mended for me.

How do you like them? Will you have them with fine or broad nibs?

Neither too fine nor too broad.

If this pen is not good, take that, and here is the pen-knife, make them yourself to your liking.

Give me a penknife, I want to mend my pen.

This penknife is good for nothing.

I have no seal; fetch me one; here is mine.

Where is the inkstand?

Will you lend me yours?

Zünden Sie ein Licht an; denn ich muß meine Briefe zusiegeln.	Light a candle; for I must seal my letters.
Ich werde nur ein Billet schreiben.	I shall only write a note.
Ich will es nur zulegen, ohne es zuzusiegeln.	I will only wrap it up, without sealing it.
Ist das Posthaus weit von hier?	Is the post-office far from here?
Tragen Sie diesen Brief auf die Post.	Take this letter to the post-office.
Heute gehet die Post nach England.	The mail sets out for England to-day.
Wie viel kostet das Postgeld für einen Brief?	How much do we pay for the postage of a letter?
Haben Sie Geld bei sich?	Have you any money by you?
Ich habe kein Kleingeld.	I have no change.
Da ist welches.	There is some.
Verlieren Sie keine Zeit, eilen Sie.	Lose no time, make haste.
Geschwind, geschwind, machen Sie fort.	Make haste, quick, look sharp.
Haben Sie meinen Brief auf die Post gegeben?	Have you taken my letter to the post-office?
War es nicht zu spät? Ist die Post abgegangen?	Was it not too late? Is the post gone?

Mit einem Tuchhändler.

WITH A WOOLLEN-DRAPER.

Mein Herr, wollen Sie mir feines Tuch zeigen?	Will you show me a fine cloth?
Welche Farbe wünschen Sie?	What colour do you want?

Soll ich Ihnen eine gemischte Farbe zeigen?	Shall I show you a mixed colour?
Nein, ich ziehe blau vor, es ist immer in der Mode.	No, I prefer blue, it is always in fashion.
Sehen Sie diese zwei Stücke. Sie sind beide in der Wolle gefärbt.	Here are two pieces, *or* look at these two pieces. They are both dyed in the wool.
Ich will beide auflegen.	I will spread them both out.
Dies Tuch scheint mir nicht weich und kernig genug.	This cloth does not seem to me soft and substantial enough.
Sie irren sich, betrachten Sie aber dieses andere Stück, vielleicht gefällt es Ihnen besser.	You are mistaken, Sir; but look at this other piece, perhaps it will suit you better.
Es ist ein sehr feines, gut geschorenes, und in der Farbe sehr solides Tuch.	It is superfine cloth, very smooth, and of a very lasting colour.
Wie hoch kommt die Elle?	How much is it a yard?
Sechs und zwanzig Schillinge.	Six and twenty shillings.
Ich erschrecke vor diesem Preise; er ist übertrieben.	That price frightens me; it is exorbitant.
Es ist ein billiger Preis. Sie sehen hier das beste Stück Tuch aller Waarenlager der Stadt.	It is a fair price. You see here the best piece of cloth of any warehouse in the town.
Schneiden Sie mir eine und drei viertel Ellen ab; dies wird hinreichend zu einem Rocke für mich seyn.	Cut me a yard and three-quarters; that will be enough to make me a coat.
Hier sind sie.	Here it is, Sir.
Haben Sie sonst nichts nöthig?	Is there nothing more you want?

Für jetzt nicht. Ich werde in zwei oder drei Tagen wiederkommen, denn ich brauche ein Paar Pantalons, und zwei Westen.

Not at present. I shall come again in two or three days, for I want a pair of pantaloons, and two waistcoats.

Mit einem Schneider.

WITH A TAILOR.

Ich habe einen Anzug nöthig, zeigen Sie mir Muster.

I want a suit of clothes, show me some patterns.

Können Sie alles dazu anschaffen?

Can you provide every thing?

Wenn Sie es verlangen.

If you wish it.

Was wollen Sie für Tuch haben?

What kind of cloth will you have?

Es muß gut seyn.

It must be good.

Ich habe alle Farben, und das feinste Tuch.

I have all kinds of colours, and the finest cloth.

Was für Farbe ist Ihnen gefällig, hell oder dunkel?

What colour would you like, light or dark?

Haben Sie keine Muster bei sich?

Have you no patterns by you?

Ja, mein Herr, hier ist eine große Karte; worin Sie eine Auswahl treffen können.

Yes, Sir; here is a large book, in which you can make your choice.

Es ist schwer, zwischen einer so großen Mannigfaltigkeit zu wählen.

It is difficult to choose out of so great a variety.

Das Schwarze ist sehr schön; ist das Tuch gut?

That black is very fine; is the cloth good?

Es kann nicht besser seyn.

There can be no better.

Dies Blau gefällt mir sehr wohl, aber die Farbe verblaßt leicht.

This blue pleases me very well; but the colour soon fades.

Ich versichere Sie, daß Ihnen ein Rock von dieser Farbe sehr gut passen wird.	I assure you that a coat of this colour will suit you very well.
Ich wähle jenes.	I shall choose that.
Wie theuer kommt es?	What is the price of it?
Drei und zwanzig Schillinge die Elle.	Three and twenty shillings an ell, *or* yard.
Das ist viel Geld, doch das Tuch ist gut.	That is a great deal of money; however, the cloth is good.
Wollen Sie mir das Maß nehmen?	Will you take my measure?
Wie wollen Sie es gemacht haben?	How will you have it made?
Wie ist jetzt die Mode?	What is the fashion now?
Es giebt mehrere; die meisten tragen hohe sammetne Kragen.	There are several; most wear high velvet collars.
Was für Knöpfe wollen Sie haben?	What buttons will you have?
Ich denke, daß vergoldete Knöpfe bei dieser Farbe gut stehen, *or* passen.	I think that gilt buttons look well with this colour.
Was denken Sie davon?	What do you think of it?
Ich überlasse das Ihrem Geschmacke.	I will leave that to your taste.
Sollen die Taschen auf der Seite oder hinten seyn?	Shall the pockets be at the side or behind?
Machen Sie mir die Taschen an der Seite.	Put the pockets at the side.
Wann glauben Sie, daß es fertig seyn wird?	When do you think it will be ready, *or* done?
Sie sollen es spätestens nächsten Sonnabend haben.	You shall have it at the latest on Saturday.

Ist das gewiß?	Is that certain?
Ich verspreche nie, was ich nicht erfüllen kann.	Sir, I never promise anything that I cannot perform.
Sie werden es aber zugeben, daß dies nicht immer die Gewohnheit bei den Herren Schneidern ist.	But you will allow that this is not always the case with gentlemen in your trade.
Ich mache es mir zur Regel, meine Kunden nie vergebens warten zu lassen, wenn es in meiner Macht stehet.	I make it a rule never to disappoint my customers, if I can possibly help it.
Gut! halten Sie aber Wort, und bringen Sie mir zugleich ihre Rechnung mit.	Very well, do not fail, and at the same time bring me your account.
Ich empfehle mich Ihnen.	Good morning, *or* good day, Sir.

Mit einem Schuhmacher.

WITH A SHOEMAKER.

Ich habe ein Paar Schuhe nöthig.	I want a pair of shoes.
Haben Sie Schuhe fertig?	Have you any shoes ready made?
Bringen Sie mir einige Paar von verschiedener Größe.	Bring me some of different sizes.
Setzen Sie sich, ich will Ihnen einige anpassen.	Sit down, I will try you some on.
Diese passen mir gar nicht, sie sind zu enge; sie drücken mich.	These do not fit me at all, they are too narrow; they pinch me.
Diese werden Ihnen besser sitzen.	These will fit you better.
Ich glaube es nicht, sie sind zu sehr ausgeschnitten und nicht hoch genug im Spann.	I do not think it; they are too low, the instep is not high enough.

Wie theuer sind diese hier? — What is the price of these?

Ich will sie anprobiren, ich glaube, sie gehen zu hoch. — I will try them; I think they come up too high.

Ich habe keine in meinem Laden, die Ihnen passen werden. — I have none in my shop that will fit you, *or* suit you.

Dann nehmen Sie mir das Maaß. — In that case take my measure.

Was wollen Sie für Leder haben? — What leather will you have?

Machen Sie sie von weichem, feinem Leder. — Make them of fine soft leather.

Sie können sich darauf verlassen, daß Sie gut bedient werden sollen. — You may rely, *or* depend upon being well served.

Wollen Sie die Spitzen rund oder stumpf haben? — Will you have round or square toes?

Die Spitzen müssen stumpf, und die Füsse lang und weit seyn. — The toes must be square, and the feet long and wide.

Und wie wünschen Sie die Stiefel? — And how do you wish to have the boots made?

Nach der Mode, mit hohen Absätzen, jedoch nicht zu hoch. — In the fashion, with high heels, but not too high.

Soll ich sie von demselben Leder wie die Schuhe machen? — Shall I make them of the same leather as the shoes?

Nein, das Leder für die Stiefel muß stark, aber nicht steif und hart seyn. — No, the leather for the boots must be stout, but not stiff and hard.

Wie soll ich die Sohlen machen, einfach oder doppelt? — How shall I make the soles, double or single?

Ich verlange blos eine einfache Sohle, welche aber dauerhaft ist. — I only wish for a single sole which is somewhat durable.

Machen Sie mir auch ein paar Pantoffeln.

Meine Stiefel und Schuhe müßen weder weit, noch enge, sondern bequem seyn — ich mag keine Hühneraugen haben.

Ich werde Sie nach Wunsch bedienen, Sie werden zufrieden seyn.

Wann wollen Sie sie mir zusenden?

Nächste Woche, verlassen Sie sich auf mein Wort.

Sehe zu, wer da ist, ich glaube, es klopft jemand.

Es ist Ihr Schumacher, soll er heraufkommen?

Ja, freilich, laß ihn hereintreten.

Make me also a pair of slippers.

My boots and shoes must be neither wide nor tight; they must be easy—I do not like to have corns.

I will serve you, Sir, as you wish,—you will be satisfied.

When will you send them to me?

Next week, depend upon my word.

See who is there, I think some one is knocking.

It is your shoemaker, Sir, shall I call him up?

Yes, to be sure, let him come in.

Mit einem Hutmacher.

Ich wollte einen Castorhut kaufen.

Wir haben welche, die sehr fein und modern sind.

Ich wünsche einen leichten Hut zu haben.

Hier ist einer, der Ihnen sehr gut stehen wird.

Diese sind leicht, und doch so stark, daß sie lange halten werden.

WITH A HATTER.

I wish to purchase a beaver hat.

We have some, which are very fine, and in fashion.

I should like to have a light hat.

Here is one that will fit you very well.

These are light, and yet so stout that they will last a long time.

Die Krone ist zu klein, er ist zu eng, und der Rand zu schmal.

Hier ist ein anderer von derselben Güte; die Form ist etwas größer.

Dieser gefällt mir; dieser ist gut; was kostet er?

Sechs und zwanzig Schillinge, das ist ein bestimmter Preis.

Das ist viel Geld.

Können Sie den Preis nicht etwas heruntersetzen?

Ich lasse nie etwas nach.

Nun gut, schicken Sie ihn mir.

Wohin soll ich ihn Ihnen schicken?

Ich will Ihnen meine Adresse geben.

Schicken Sie mir ihn unfehlbar morgen früh.

Ich werde nicht verfehlen, Sie können sich darauf verlassen.

Mit einem Strumpfhändler.

Wollen Sie mit mir kommen?

Wohin haben Sie Lust zu gehen?

Ich möchte zu einem Strumpf= händler gehen.

Ich habe in einem Laden recht schöne Strümpfe gesehen, die mir sehr gefallen.

The crown is too small, it is too tight, and the brim too small.

Here is another of the same quality; the shape is somewhat larger.

I like this; this will do; what is the price?

Six and twenty shillings, that is a fixed price.

That is a great deal of money.

Can you not take something off?

I never abate anything.

Well then, send it to me.

Where shall I send it to you?

I will give you my address.

Do not fail to send it me to-morrow morning.

I will not fail, you may depend upon it.

WITH A HOSIER.

Will you come with me?

Where do you wish to go?

I want to go to a hosier's.

I have seen some very fine stockings in a shop, which please me very much.

Für wie viel verkaufen Sie diese Strümpfe?	How much do you sell these stockings for?
Ich verkaufe das Paar zu zwölf Schillinge.	I sell them for twelve shillings a pair.
Denken Sie nicht, daß das zu theuer ist?	Don't you think that that is too dear?
Erwägen Sie, daß sie schwer und sehr fein sind.	Consider, they are heavy and very fine.
Das gebe ich zu, aber die Farbe gefällt mir nicht.	I grant that, but the colour does not please me.
Hier sind andere, Sie können wählen.	Here are others, you may choose.
Diese gefallen mir recht gut; wie verkaufen Sie die?	These please me very well; how do you sell them?
Sie sind alle von einerlei Preise.	They are all of the same price.
Ich will Ihnen zehn Schillinge dafür geben.	I will give you ten shillings for them.
Ich lasse nie etwas ab; ich habe Ihnen meinen genauesten Preis gesagt.	I never abate any thing; I have told you my lowest price.
Das sagen alle Handelsleute.	That is what all shopkeepers say.
Ich gebe nicht mehr als zehn Schillinge.	I shall only give ten shillings.
Dann hoffe ich aber, daß Sie mir Ihre Kundschaft ein andermal gönnen werden.	I hope, then, that you will favour me with your custom another time.
Davon können Sie überzeugt seyn; ich werde Ihnen auch andere Kunden verschaffen.	You may rely upon it; I will even procure you other customers.
Ich werde Ihnen dafür sehr verbunden seyn.	I shall be very much obliged to you for it.

Mit einem Haarschneider.

Ich muß einen Haarschneider, oder einen Barbier haben.
Sagen Sie dem Barbier, er soll sogleich herkommen.
Wollen Sie mich gefälligst rasiren?
Sind Ihre Rasiermesser gut?
Nehmen Sie sich in Acht, daß Sie mich nicht schneiden.
Machen Sie geschwind, ich bitte.
Soll ich Ihre Haare schneiden.
Ja, Sie müssen mir die Haare schneiden und frisiren.
Ihre Haare locken sich sehr gut.
Ist das Eisen nicht zu heiß? Probieren Sie es erst auf Papier.
Wo sind Ihre Kämme?
Machen Sie mir große Haarlocken, damit ich geschwinder fertig werde.
Nehmen Sie den weiten Kamm.
Drücken Sie nicht so stark auf, Sie thun mir wehe.
Diese Locke sitzt schlecht.
Soll ich ein wenig Pomade in Ihre Haare thun?
Nein, so ist es gut.

WITH A HAIR-DRESSER, &c.

I must have a hair-dresser, or barber.
Tell the barber to come directly.
Will you have the kindness to shave me?
Are your razors good?
Take care not to cut me, or that you do not cut me.
Pray make haste.
Shall I cut your hair?
Yes, you must cut my hair and curl it.
Your hair curls very well.
Is not that iron too hot? Try it first upon paper.
Where are your combs?
Make the curls large, that it may be sooner done.
Take the large comb.
Do not press so hard, you hurt me.
This curl does not lie well.
Shall I put a little pomatum on your hair?
No, that will do.

Mit einem Zahnarzte.

Ich habe Zahnschmerzen.
Mir thut der Zahn sehr weh.

WITH A DENTIST.

I have the tooth-ache.
My tooth aches very much.

Das ist schlimm; haben Sie einen verborbenen Zahn?
Ich glaube, dieser Schmerz rührt von einem verborbenen Zahne her.
Der Schmerz wird sich bald verlieren.
Das wäre mir sehr lieb.
Wollen Sie meinen Mund untersuchen?
Sie haben einen hohlen Zahn.
Sie haben zwei verborbene Zähne.
Kann man sie plombiren?

Ich will sie plombiren, wenn Sie es wünschen.

Das Zahnfleisch ist geschwollen.
Wollen Sie diesen Zahn ausziehen?
Nein; man muß ihn nicht ausziehen, so lange Sie eine geschwollene Backe haben.
Was soll ich denn thun, um den Schmerz zu lindern?
Stecken Sie in den hohlen Zahn ein wenig Baumwolle, in Aether getaucht.
Sollte Nelkenöhl oder Zimmetöhl meinen Schmerz nicht lindern?
Ja, aber Aether ist weit besser.

That is bad; have you a bad, *or* decayed tooth?
I think this pain proceeds from a bad, *or* decayed tooth.
The pain will soon be over, *or* soon cease.
I am very glad to hear it.
Will you examine my mouth?
You have a hollow tooth.
You have two decayed teeth.
Can they be filled up with lead?
I will fill them up with lead if you like, *or* if you wish it.
The gums are swelled.
Will you pull out this tooth?
No; it must not be pulled out so long as your cheek continues swollen.
What must I do, then, to allay the pain?
Put a little cotton dipt in æther into the hollow tooth.
Would not oil of cloves or cinnamon ease the pain?
Yes, but æther is much better.

Mit einem Uhrmacher.	**WITH A WATCH-MAKER.**
Ich wollte gerne eine Uhr kaufen.	I want to purchase a watch.
Was für eine wollen Sie haben?	What kind would you please to have?
Ich möchte gern eine goldene Uhr haben.	I should like to have a gold watch.
Ich habe allerlei Sorten.	I have of all kinds.
Ist diese Uhr gut?	Is this a good one?
Ja wohl, diese kann ich Ihnen empfehlen.	Yes, Sir, I can recommend this to you.
Wollen Sie sie mir auf Probe geben?	Will you let me have it upon trial?
Wenn Sie es besonders verlangen.	If you particularly wish it.
Ich werde sie mir unter dieser Bedingung kaufen.	I will only buy it on these conditions.
Wie viel kostet sie?	What is the price?
Der Preis ist fünfzehn Guineen.	The price is fifteen guineas.
Sie fordern zu viel, sie ist viel zu theuer.	You ask too much, it is much too dear.
Ich gebe Ihnen zwölf, und bezahle Sie in einem Monate.	I will give you twelve, and pay you in a month.
Es ist sehr wenig.	It, *or* that is very little.
Ich wollte gerne meine Uhr vertauschen.	I should like to exchange my watch.
Wie viel wollen Sie zu haben?	How much do you want in exchange?
Ich kann nicht weniger als fünf Guineen zunehmen.	I cannot take less than five guineas in exchange.
Ich will es Ihnen geben.	I will give it you.
Wie heißt der Uhrmacher?	What is the maker's name?
Ich habe mein Uhrglas zerbrochen.	I have broken my watch-glass.

Ich muß ein neues Glas einsetzen lassen, und habe außerdem die Feder zerbrochen.
Was fehlt ihr? Erlauben Sie mir gefälligst zu sehen.
Sie muß gereinigt werden.
Ich bitte Sie, sie zu reinigen, und zurecht zu machen, und mir unterdessen eine andere zu leihen.

I must get a new glass put to it, besides I have broken the main spring.
What is the matter with it? Allow me to look at it.
It wants cleaning.
I beg you to clean it, and put it right again, and in the mean time to lend me another.

Mit einem Juwelier.

WITH A JEWELLER.

Was wünschen Sie zu kaufen?
Ich wünsche eine Uhrkette zu kaufen.
Wie viel kostet diese goldene Kette?
Zehn Guineen, und dieser Preis ist sehr billig.
Das ist sehr theuer. Ich gebe Ihnen acht.
Es ist sehr wenig; da Sie jedoch einer meiner Kunten sind, so will ich sie Ihnen um diesen Preis erlassen.
Wie theuer ist diese Nadel und dieses Petschaft?
Haben Sie Tabaksdosen?
Haben Sie einen Diamant?
Hier ist ein Brilliant von sechs und einem halben Gran.
Es ist Schade, daß er ein wenig Farbe hat.

What do you wish to buy?
I wish to purchase a watch-chain.
What is the price of this gold chain?
Ten guineas, and that is very reasonable.
That is very dear, I will give you eight.
That is very little; but as you are one of my customers, I must let you have it at that price.
What is the price of this pin and seal?
Have you any snuff-boxes?
Have you a diamond?
Here is a brilliant of six grains and a half.
It is a pity that it has a little colour.

Wäre er von schönstem Wasser, so würde er hundert Guineen werth seyn.	If it were of the finest water, it would be worth a hundred guineas.
Ich wünsche einen Diamant, der Staat macht und wenig kostet.	I want a diamond that makes a great show, and costs little.
Dieser ist gerade, was Sie suchen.	Then this is just the thing you want.
Sagen Sie mir den äußersten Preis, und ich werde sehen, ob er mir ansteht.	Tell me the lowest price, and I will see whether it suits me.
Meine Gattin braucht Ohrringe und Armbänder; sie wird aber selbst kommen, zu wählen.	My wife wants some earrings and bracelets, but she will come and choose for herself.
Ich werde mich bemühen, sie nach ihrem Geschmacke zu bedienen. Unterdessen haben Sie die Güte ihr meine Empfehlung zu geben.	I will do all I can to serve her to her taste. In the mean time I beg you will have the kindnes to present my respects to her.

Um Erkundigungen einzuziehen, bevor man eine Reise unternimmt.

TO MAKE ENQUIRIES BEFORE UNDERTAKING A JOURNEY.

Wie viel Meilen sind es von hier nach Berlin?	How many miles is it from here to Berlin?
Hundert Meilen.	A hundred miles.
Wie viel Stunden macht dies?	How many leagues is that?
Zwei hundert.	Two hundred.
Sind die Wege gut?	Are the roads good?

Observe—The German mile equals about four and two-fifths English miles, and the Stunde, (literally *hour*) equals half a German mile, or about two and a quarter miles English.

Sie sind weder gut noch schlecht.	They are neither good nor bad.
Bald gut bald schlecht.	Sometimes good and sometimes bad.
Es ist sehr sandig.	It is very sandy.
Gibt es viele Geleise?	Are there many ruts?
Ja, in einigen Gegenden.	Yes, in some places.
Gibt es viele Berge?	Are there many mountains?
Ja, es sind viele Berge, Wälder und Abgründe da.	Yes, there are many mountains, forests, and precipices.
Ist der Weg breit?	Is the road broad?
Ja, ziemlich breit.	Yes, tolerably broad.
Nein, ziemlich schmal.	No, rather narrow.
Die Gegend, durch welche Sie kommen werden, ist ganz eben.	The country through which you will pass, is quite flat, or level.
Sind die Gasthöfe gut?	Are the inns good?
So ziemlich. Sie sind leidlich.	Tolerable. They are midling.
Es gibt gute und schlechte.	There are good and bad.
Wollen Sie wohl die Güte haben, mir die besten anzuzeigen?	Will you have the kindness to point out the best to me?
Wollen Sie es wohl in mein Taschenbuch schreiben; hier ist ein Bleistift.	Will you be so good as to write it down in my pocket-book; here is a pencil.
Sind die Betten rein?	Are the beds clean?
An einigen Orten, ja; an andern nicht.	In some places they are; in others not.
Kann man leicht frische Betttücher bekommen?	Can you easily get clean sheets?

Manchmal hat man Mühe welche zu erhalten.	Frequently it is difficult to get them.
Welche Städte findet man auf dem Wege?	What towns are there on the road?
Mehrere; es lohnet sich aber nicht der Mühe sich deshalb aufzuhalten.	There are several; but they are not worth stopping at.
Wie viel Tage braucht man bis S.?	How many days does it take to go to S.?
Fünf Tage mit dem Postwagen, und vier mit Extrapost.	Five days by the coach, and four by the post.
Lebt man theuer in den Gasthöfen?	Is it expensive living at the inn?
Die Mahlzeit kostet ungefähr vier Franken.	It costs about four franks a meal.
Ich habe meinen eigenen Wagen; könnte ich Miethpferde zu billigem Preise finden?	I have my own carriage; can I hire horses at a reasonable price?
Man findet hier leicht welche.	You may easily get them here.
Wie viel zahlt man für das Pferd?	How much do you pay for each horse?
Ich weiß es nicht; Sie können es aber im Postbuch finden.	I do not know, but you can find it in the post-book.
Wie viel giebt man dem Postillion?	How much do you give the postillion?
Gewöhnlich dreißig Kreuzer für die Station; ist man aber zufrieden mit ihm, so gibt man ihm einige Kreuzer mehr.	Usually thirty kreutzers a post; but if you are satisfied with him, you may give him a few kreutzers more.

Observe.—The value of a kreutzer is rather more than the third of a penny.

Im Begriffe, die Reise anzutreten.	JUST ON SETTING OUT.
Sind die Pferde da?	Are the horses come?
Ja, mein Herr, sie sind hier.	Yes, Sir; they are here.
So laßt schnell anspannen, denn wir wollen sogleich abreisen.	Let them be put to directly, for we wish to set off immediately.
Sie sind schon angespannt.	They are to already.
Johann, laß den Kutscher vorfahren.	John, tell the coachman to draw up.
Er ist schon da.	He is at the door.
Ist der Koffer gut befestiget?	Is the trunk well fastened?
Ja, mein Herr, die Stricke sind tüchtig zusammengezogen.	Yes, Sir; it is tied quite tight.
Hast du die Kette nicht darum befestiget?	Have not you put the chain to it?
Ja mein Herr, vor allen Dingen.	Yes, Sir; that was the first thing we did.
Ich möchte nicht, daß man uns den Koffer unter Wegs stähle.	I should not like the trunk to be stolen on the road.
Es hat keine Gefahr.	There is no danger.
Sehe in allen Zimmern nach, daß nichts vergessen wird.	Look into all the rooms, that nothing may be forgotten.
Ich habe dies schon überall, gethan; es ist nichts vergessen.	I have already done so; nothing is forgotten.
Lassen Sie uns gehen, meine Herren? es ist Zeit abzureisen.	Let us go, gentlemen, it is time to set off.
Nehme diese beiden Hüte, und befestige sie in dem Netze.	Take these two hats, and put them into the net.

Lege diesen Regenschirm und die Schuhe und Stiefeln in den Wagenkasten.
Put this umbrella, the shoes and boots into the boot of the carriage.

Aber, was sollen wir mit diesen Büchern machen?
But what shall we do with these books?

Wir wollen sie selbst mit herunter nehmen, und in die Wagentaschen stecken.
We will take them down ourselves, and put them into the pockets.

Höre, Postillion, du fährst langsam, wenn der Weg schlecht ist.
Postillion, mind you drive slowly when the road is bad.

Ich werde Ihre Befehle befolgen.
Sir, I shall obey your orders.

Johann, öffne den Schlag, und laß den Fußtritt herunter.
John, open the door and let the step down.

Reisen Sie glücklich, meine Herren.
Gentlemen, I wish you a good journey.

Die Stunden, u.s.w.

THE HOURS, &c.

Wie viel Uhr ist es?
What o'clock is it?

Sagen Sie mir gefälligst, wie viel Uhr es ist.
Tell me what o'clock it is, if you please.

Es ist zwölf Uhr, oder Mittag.
It is twelve o'clock, *or* noon.

Es ist ein Viertel auf eins, *or* Es ist ein Viertel nach zwölf.
It is a quarter past twelve.

Es ist halb eins, *or* es ist halb ein Uhr.
It is half past twelve.

Es ist drei Viertel auf eins.
It wants a quarter to one.

Es ist ein Uhr.
It is one o'clock.

Es ist ein Viertel nach eins, *or* Es ist ein Viertel auf zwei.
It is a quarter past one.

Es ist halb zwei.
It is half past one.

Es ist drei Viertel auf zwei.
It wants a quarter to two.

Es fehlen zehn Minuten zu zwei, *or* Es ist fünfzig Minuten nach eins.

Es ist zehn Minuten vor zwei.

Es ist ein Viertel auf drei.

Es ist zwanzig Minuten nach zwei.

Wie viel fehlt es zu drei, *or* Wie viel ist es auf drei?

Es hat schon drei Uhr geschlagen.

Es ist schon drei Uhr.

Um wie viel Uhr gehen Sie?

Ich gehe um fünf Uhr.

Es schlug eben fünf, *or* es schlug eben fünf Uhr.

Sehen Sie, welche Zeit es nach Ihrer Uhr ist.

Meine Uhr geht zu geschwinde.

Und die meinige geht zu langsam.

Sie ist seit zwei Tagen nicht im Gange gewesen.

Wissen Sie, wie viel die Uhr ist?

Ich denke, es ist ungefähr acht Uhr.

Ich weiß nicht, welche Zeit es ist, meine Uhr ist abgelaufen.

Es wird bald acht schlagen.

Hat es schon geschlagen?

Wie viel schlägt es jetzt?

Ich habe die Glocke nicht gehört.

Es kann auf den Schlag neun seyn.

It wants ten minutes to two.

It is ten minutes to two.

It is a quarter past two.

It is twenty minutes past two.

How much does it want to three?

It has already struck three.

It is already three o'clock.

At what o'clock do you go?

I go about five o'clock.

It struck five just now.

Look what o'clock it is by your watch.

My watch goes too fast.

And mine goes too slow.

It has not gone for these two days.

Do you know what o'clock it is?

I think it is about eight o'clock.

I do not know what o'clock it is, my watch is down.

It will soon strike eight.

Has it already struck?

What is it striking now?

I have not heard the clock.

It may be on the stroke of nine.

Es ist auf den Schlag neun. — It is on the stroke of nine.

Ich glaube nicht, daß es so spät ist. — I do not think that it is so late.

Horch, die Glocke schlägt jetzt. — Listen, the clock is striking now.

Ja, ich dachte, es wäre später. — Yes, I thought it might be later.

Das ist Ihre Zeit zu Frühstücken nicht wahr? — That is your time for breakfasting, is it not?

Nach dem Wege fragen. — TO ASK THE WAY.

Ist es weit von hier nach der Königsstraße? — Is it far from here to King's Street?

Ist dieß der rechte Weg nach der Kronenstraße? — Is this the right way to Crown Street?

Ja, mein Herr, gehen Sie gerade aus, und am Ende der Straße, wenden Sie sich zur rechten Hand. — Yes, Sir; go straight along, an at the end of the street, turn to the right hand.

Wollten Sie wohl die Güte haben, und mir sagen ob ich weit von der Londonstraße bin? — Would you have the goodness to tell me whether I am far from London Street?

Nach welcher Seite muß ich gehen? — Which way must I go?

Muß ich hernach rechts oder links umwenden? — Must I afterwards turn to the right or the left?

Wohnt Herr P. hier? — Does Mr. P. live here?

Kennen Sie den Herren G. den Banquier? or Ist Ihnen Herr G. der Geldwechsler bekannt? — Do you know Mr. G., the Banker?

Ja, mein Herr, ich kenne ihn. — Yes, Sir; I know him.

Wollten Sie mir wohl seine Addresse geben?	Will you favour me with his address?
Ja, er wohnt in der nächsten Straße, an der linken Hand.	Yes, he lives in the next street, on the left hand side.
Könnten Sie mir wohl sagen welchen Weg ich nehmen muß um zu......zu kommen?	Can you tell which way I must take in order to go to......
Führen Sie mich den kürzesten Weg.	Show me the shortest way.
Rufen Sie mir einen Miethkutscher.	Call me a hackney-coach.
Kutscher, fahren Sie mich nach Walworth.	Coachman, drive me to Walworth.

Beim Aufstehen am Morgen.

ON GETTING UP IN THE MORNING.

Wer ist da?	Who is there?
Wer klopft an die Thür?	Who knocks at the door?
Sind Sie noch im Bette?	Are you still in bed?
Sind Sie eingeschlafen?	Are you asleep?
Schlafen Sie noch?	Are you still asleep?
Wachen Sie auf. Stehen Sie auf.	Awake. Get up.
Ich wache schon.	I am already awake.
Wer hat Sie geweckt?	Who has awaked you?
Mein Bruder. Meine Schwester.	My brother. My sister.
Ist es Zeit aufzustehen?	Is it time to get up?
Ja, es ist heller Tag.	Yes, it is broad day-light
Es ist acht Uhr.	It is eight o'clock.
Es ist noch zu früh.	It is yet too early.
Ganz und gar nicht.	Not at all.
Machen Sie die Thür auf.	Open the door.

Warten Sie ein wenig.	Wait a little.
Sie ist zugeschlossen.	It is locked.
Sie ist verriegelt.	It is bolted.
Ich werde gleich aufstehen.	I am going to get up directly.
Ich stehe eben auf.	I am just getting up.
Ich dachte nicht, daß es schon so spät wäre.	I did not think it was so late.
Warum ziehen Sie sich nicht an?	Why do you not dress yourself?
Ziehen Sie sich geschwind an.	Make haste and dress yourself.
Ich muß meine Hände waschen.	I must wash my hands.
Geben Sie mir das Waschbecken.	Give me the wash-hand basin.
Geben Sie mir ein wenig Seife.	Give me a little soap.
Meine Hände sind sehr schmutzig.	My hands are very dirty.
Ich werde mich nicht lange anziehen.	I shall not be long dressing myself.
Wo ist mein Hemd? Hier ist es.	Where is my shirt? Here it is.
Dies Hemd ist nicht rein.	This shirt is not clean.
Geben Sie mir ein Taschentuch.	Give me a pocket-handkerchief.
Sie sollten jetzt schon in der Schule seyn.	You should be in the school now.
Ihre Mitschüler spielen im Hofe.	Your school-fellows are playing in the yard.
Sie sind fleißiger als Sie.	They are more diligent than you.
Jemehr ich schlafe, desto mehr bedarf ich des Schlafes.	The more I sleep, the more I want to sleep.

Ehe man zu Bette geht.	BEFORE GOING TO BED.
Die Nacht kommt heran.	Night is coming on.
Die Nacht nähert sich.	Night approaches.
Es fängt an finster zu werden; es ist sehr spät.	It is beginning to grow dark; it is very late.
Es ist Zeit zu Bette zu gehen.	It is time to go to bed.
Ich gehe zeitig zu Bette.	I go to bed early.
Ich will zu Bette gehen.	I will go to bed.
Bringen Sie mir den Stiefelknecht und Pantoffeln.	Bring me the boot-jack and slippers.
Kommen Sie mit mir, und wärmen Sie mein Bett.	Come with me, and warm my bed.
Ist mein Bett gemacht?	Is my bed made?
Haben Sie mir mein Bett gemacht?	Have you made my bed?
Es ist gut gemacht.	It is well made.
Sie müssen das Bett noch einmal machen; Sie haben es schlecht gemacht.	You must make the bed again, you have made it badly.
Lassen Sie es wärmen.	Let it be warmed.
Wo ist der Bettwärmer?	Where is the warming-pan?
Geben Sie mir eine Schlafmütze.	Give me a night-cap.
Kleiden Sie sich aus.	Undress yourself.
Ziehen Sie Ihre Schuhe und Strümpfe aus.	Pull off your shoes and stockings.
Helfen Sie mir, meinen Rock auszziehen.	Help me to pull off my coat.
Kommen Sie bald das Licht zu holen.	Come soon to fetch the light.
Dieser Leuchter ist sehr schmutzig.	This candlestick is very dirty.
Lassen Sie das Licht da.	Leave the candle there.
Ich werde es auslöschen.	I will put it out, *or* extinguish it.

Ziehen Sie die Vorhänge zu.
Nehmen Sie das Licht weg.
Guten Abend. Gute Nacht.
Wecken Sie mich doch morgen
zeitig.
Ja, ich werde Sie wecken.
Um wie viel Uhr pflegen Sie
aufzustehen?
Ich muß mit Tagesanbruch auf=
stehen, um sieben Uhr.

Beim Ankleiden.

Wo sind meine Strümpfe?
Welche meinen Sie?
Geben Sie mir die baumwollene
Strümpfe.
Was suchen Sie?
Ich suche meine Strumpfbänder.
Werden Sie sich heute rasiren?
Nein, ich habe mich gestern
rasirt, und werde mich nun
erst wieder morgen rasiren.
Geben Sie mir meine Pantoffeln.
Sie stehen bei Ihrem Bette.
Bringen Sie mir das Wasch=
becken und ein wenig Seife.
Geben Sie mir das Handtuch.
Wollen Sie ein reines Hemd?
Allerdings; auch ein reines
Halstuch geben Sie mir.
Wollen Sie Stiefel oder Schuhe?

Was ist es für Wetter?

Draw the curtains.
Take away the candle.
Good evening. Good night.
Wake me early in the morning.
Yes, I will awake you.
At what o'clock do you usually rise?
I must get up at day-break, about seven o'clock.

ON DRESSING.

Where are my stockings?
Which do you mean?
Give me the cotton stockings.
What are you looking for?
I am looking for my garters.
Will you shave to-day?
No, I shaved myself yesterday, and shall not shave again till to-morrow.
Give me my slippers.
They are by your bed.
Bring me the wash-hand basin, and a little soap.
Give me the towel.
Will you have a clean shirt?
Certainly, and a clean neckcloth too.
Will you have boots or shoes?
How is the weather?

Es ist schlechtes Wetter, Herr, es regnet.	It is bad weather, Sir, it rains.
Geben Sie mir meine Stiefel, da die Straßen schmutzig seyn müssen.	Give me my boots, as the streets must be dirty.
Bürste mir den Schmutz von den Stiefeln.	Brush the dirt off the boots.
Lassen Sie meine Schuhe ausbessern.	Get my shoes mended.
Meine Stiefel sind nicht blank geworden.	My boots have not been polished, *or* cleaned.
Hat die Wäscherin mein Leinenzeug (Wäsche) gebracht?	Has the washerwoman brought my linen?
Nein, Herr, noch nicht; aber sie wird es heute bringen.	No, Sir, not yet; but she will bring it to-day.
Bürsten Sie meine Kleider gut aus.	Brush my clothes well.
Hier ist die Bürste.	Here is the brush.
Bringen Sie mir meine Handschuhe, meinen Hut, meinen Stock, meinen Regenschirm, und meinen Ueberrock.	Bring me my gloves, my hat, my stick, my umbrella, and my great-coat.

Zwischen einer Dame und ihrer Kammerjungfer. — BETWEEN A LADY AND HER WAITING-MAID.

Marie, kommen Sie her.	Maria, come here
Rufen Sie, Madame?	Do you call, Ma'am?
Ja, wie viel Uhr ist es?	Yes, what o'clock is it?
Ich weiß es nicht, Madame.	I do not know, Ma'am.
Sehen Sie auf meine Uhr.	Look at my watch.
Sie geht nicht, sie ist abgelaufen.	It does not go, it is down.
Geben Sie sie mir, damit ich sie aufziehen kann.	Give it to me, that I may wind it up.
Hier ist sie, Madame.	Here it is, Ma'am.

Es hat schon zehn Uhr geschlagen. It has already struck ten.
Haben Sie es schlagen hören? Did you hear it strike?
Ich glaube, es ist nicht so spät. I think it is not so late.
Reinigen Sie ein wenig diesen Spiegel, er ist ganz trübe. Clean this looking-glass a little, it is quite dull.
Wo ist meine Zahnbürste? Where is my tooth-brush?
Ich kann sie nicht finden. I cannot find it.
Suchen Sie sie. Look for it.
Ich suche sie überall. I am looking for it every where.

Sie lassen alle Dinge in Unordnung. You leave every thing in disorder.
Reinigen Sie meine Kämme. Clean my combs.
Sie sind rein, Madame. They are clean, Ma'am.
Geben Sie mir eine Stecknadel. Give me a pin.
Wo ist das Nadelküssen? Where is the pincushion?
Sehen Sie zu ob mein Halstuch hinten gerade sitzt. Look whether my handkerchief is straight behind.
Stecken Sie es mit einer Nadel an. Fasten it with a pin, *or* pin it fast.
Sie stechen mich. You are pricking me.
Geben Sie mir einen Stuhl. Give me a chair.
Nehmen Sie diesen Spiegel weg. Take away that glass.
Geben Sie mir eine Schere. Give me a pair of scissors.
Thun Sie mir mein Halsband um, und geben Sie mir meine Ohrringe. Put on my necklace, and give me my ear-rings.
Geben Sie mir meinen Muff und meinen Fächer. Give me my muff and fan.

Mit einer Wäscherin. WITH A WASHER-WOMAN.

Werden Sie mir Ihre schmutzige Wäsche heute übergeben? Will you give me out your dirty linen to-day?
Nein; kommen Sie morgen. No; come to-morrow.

Wann werden Sie meine Wäsche wiederbringen?	When shall you bring my linen back again?
Am Sonnabend gewiß.	On Saturday without fail.
Ich bitte Sie, sie mit vielem Fleiße zu waschen.	I beg you will wash it carefully.
Ich bitte Sie, keine Stärke daran zu thun, wenn Sie meine Nachthauben waschen.	Pray do not use any starch when you wash my nightcaps.
Dieses Kleid muß gewaschen und gebügelt werden.	This gown must be washed and ironed.
Meine Strümpfe müssen ausgebessert werden. Können Sie sie ausbessern?	My stockings must be mended. Can you mend them?
Nein, mein Herr, ich kann sie nicht ausbessern.	No, Sir, I cannot mend them.
Kennen Sie jemand, der seidene Strümpfe ausbessern kann?	Do you know any one, who can mend silk stockings?
Bringen Sie Ihre Rechnung mit.	Bring your bill with you.
Bringen Sie schon meine Wäsche?	Are you bringing my linen already?
Laßt sehen, ob mein Weißzeug rein ist.	Let me see, whether my linen is clean.
Sehen Sie, Herr, Ihre Wäsche ist sehr weiß und gut gebügelt.	Look, Sir, your linen is very white and well ironed.
Nein, meine Hemden sind zu blau. Ich verlange sie schneeweiß und die Falten feiner.	No, my shirts are too blue. I want them as white as snow and the plaits finer.
Diese Falten sind schlecht gemacht. Dies ist schlecht geplättet.	These plaits are not well done. This is badly ironed.
Dies ist nicht recht gewaschen	This is not well washed.

Ich thue indessen mein möglich=
   stes, um sie gut zu bedienen,
   und Sie zufrieden zu stellen.
Ich will meine Wäsche über=
   zählen.
Drei Paar Betttücher.
Vierzehn Hemden.
Zwei Unterröcke und ein Kleid.
Fünf Paar Strümpfe.
Sechs Paar Socken.
Ein Paar Unterbeinkleider, *or*
   Unterhosen.
Vier Nachthauben, *or* Nacht=
   mützen.
Sechs Halsbinden.
Zwei Halstücher.
Ein Paar Handschuhe.
Sieben Schnupftücher, *or* Ta=
   schentücher.
Zwei Tischtücher.
Acht Handtücher.
Fünfzehn Servietten.
Es fehlen zwei Handtücher.

Zehn Schürzen.
Zwei Corsetten.
Drei Schawle.
Ein Paar Taschen.
Da ist ein Schnupftuch, welches
   nicht mir gehört. Es ist nicht
   mein Zeichen.
Bringen Sie Ihre Rechnung, und
   ich werde alles bezahlen, was
   ich Ihnen schuldig bin.

I do every thing I can, however, to please you, and
   make you satisfied.
I will count over my linen.

Three pairs of sheets.
Fourteen shirts.
Two petticoats, and one gown
Five pairs of stockings.
Six pairs of socks.
One pair of drawers.

Four nightcaps.

Six cravats.
Two neckhandkerchiefs.
A pair of gloves.
Seven pocket-handkerchiefs.

Two table-cloths.
Eight towels.
Fifteen table-napkins.
There are two towels want-
   ing.
Ten aprons.
Two pairs of stays.
Three shawls.
A pair of pockets.
There is a handkerchief
   which does not belong to
   me. It is not my mark.
Bring your account, and I
   will pay you what I owe
   you, *or* am indebted to you.

Einen Besuch zu machen.

Es klopft jemand an die Thür.
Sehen Sie, wer es ist.
Oefnen Sie die Thür.
Es ist Frau und Herr R.
Wie befinden Sie sich, Madame?
Sehr wohl, ich danke Ihnen, und wie befinden Sie sich?
Ziemlich wohl, ich danke Ihnen.

Wir freuen uns alle sehr, Sie zu sehen.
Ich habe Sie sehr lange nicht gesehen.
Sie machen sich sehr rar.
Wann sind Sie abgereiset?
Diesen Morgen um sechs Uhr.

Es ist etwas außerordentliches Sie zu sehen.
Bitte, setzen Sie sich.
Reiche der Frau R. einen Stuhl.
Gib dem Herrn einen Stuhl.
Nein, ich danke; bemühen Sie sich nicht, ich muß Sie verlassen.
Ich muß gehen, es ist spät.
Ich habe um eilf Uhr eine Zusammenkunft, und es ist schon halb eilf.

PAYING A VISIT.

Some one knocks at the door.
Look, or see, who it is.
Open the door.
It is Mr. and Mrs. R.
How do you do, Ma'am?
Very well, thank you, and how do you do?
Tolerable, *or* pretty well, thank you.

We are all very glad to see you.
I have not seen you this age, *or* for a long time.
You are quite a stranger.
When did you set out?
This morning about six o'clock.

It is quite a favor to see you.

Pray be seated.
Give Mrs. R. a chair.
Give the Gentleman a chair.
No, thank you, do not trouble yourself, I must leave you.

I must go, it is late.
I have an engagement at eleven o'clock, and it is already half-past ten.

Haben Sie die Güte, sich nur auf zwei Minuten zu setzen; Sie kommen so selten zu mir.	Have the kindness to sit down only for two minutes; you so seldom come to see me.
Ich kann nicht bleiben.	I cannot stay.
Sie sind sehr eilig.	You are in a great hurry.
Ich habe viel zu thun.	I have a great deal to do.
Ich wünsche Ihnen einen guten Morgen.	I wish you a good morning.
Es ist mir sehr angenehm, Sie so wohl zu finden.	I am happy to see you looking so well.
Ich befinde mich sehr wohl, Gott sei Dank.	I am very well, thank God.
Ich habe gerade diesen Morgen Hrn. M. nach Ihrem Befinden gefragt.	I was just enquiring after you this morning from Mr. M.
Ich danke Ihnen für Ihre Aufmerksamkeit.	I thank you for your kind attention.
Wie befindet sich Ihre Frau Gemahlin?	How is your lady?
Seit einigen Tagen befindet sie sich nicht ganz wohl.	She has not been very well for some days.
Ich höre dies mit Bedauern.	I am very sorry to hear it.
Nähern Sie sich dem Feuer um sich zu trocknen, es ist ein so starker Nebel, daß Sie bestimmt frieren müssen.	Come nearer the fire to dry yourself, there is so thick a fog, that you must be cold.
Nein, ich friere nicht. Wenn auch das Wetter neblicht ist, so ist es doch auch sehr mild.	No, Sir, I am not cold. Though the weather is cloudy, it is nevertheless very mild.
Ich muß jetzt gehen.	I must go now.
Sie können gewiß noch ein wenig bleiben.	Surely you can stay a little longer.

Ich will ein andermal länger verweilen; ich muß noch bei vielen ansprechen.	I will stay longer another time; I have many places to call at.
Wir werden uns heute Abend da sehen, wo wir uns gewöhnlich treffen.	I shall see you again this evening, where we usually meet.
Ja, ich werde hingehen, besonders weil ich Herrn N. sprechen muß.	Yes, I shall go there, particularly as I wish to speak to Mr. N.
Ich danke Ihnen für Ihren Besuch.	I thank you for your visit.
Ich hoffe Sie bald wiederzusehen.	I hope I shall soon see you again.
Empfehlen Sie mich Ihrer Frau Gemahlin.	Present my respects to your lady.

Beim Whistspiel. AT WHIST.

Fordern Sie Karten.	Call for, *or* order cards.
Wollen Sie Whist spielen?	Will you play at whist?
Ich spiele schlecht.	I play but badly.
Wie hoch spielen Sie?	How high do you play?
Nicht sehr hoch.	Not very high.
Wer gibt?	Who is to deal?
Ich gebe; muß ich die Karten mischen?	I am to deal; must I shuffle the cards?
Wollen Sie gefälligst abheben?	Will you cut, if you please?
Ich habe eben abgehoben.	I have just cut.
Haben Sie die Karten gemischt?	Have you shuffled the cards?
Ja, Madame, und ich habe eben gegeben.	Yes, Ma'am, and I have just dealt.
Ich bitte um Verzeihung, mein Herr, Sie haben nicht recht gegeben; ich habe nur zwölf Karten.	I beg your pardon, Sir, you have dealt wrong, *or* you have lost the deal, I have only twelve cards.

Ja, Madame, ich habe unrecht gegeben.	Yes, Ma'am, I have dealt wrong.
Eine Karte ist umgelegt; es muß noch einmal gegeben werden.	One card is turned up; you must deal again.
Wer hat die Vorhand?	Who has the lead?
Ich habe die Vorhand.	I have the lead.
Der Herr hat Rauten (Careaux) ausgespielt.	This gentleman has played diamonds.
Was ist Trumpf?	What are trumps?
Herz ist Trumpf	Hearts are trumps.
Ich werde einen Trumpf ausspielen.	I shall play a trump.
Ich habe ihn getrumpft.	I have trumped him.
Sie haben Farbe verläugnet.	You have revoked.
Jetzt gebe ich.	I am to deal now.
Wir haben die Lese verloren.	We have lost the odd trick.
Wir wollen die Stellen wechseln.	We will change places.
Die Karten sind nicht gut gemischt.	The cards are not well shuffled.
Heben Sie gefälligst ab.	Cut them if you please.
Wer hat den König ausgespielt?	Who played the king?
Es ist gegen Sie.	It is against you.
Wer spielte die Königin aus?	Who played the queen?
Ich, Madame.	I played it, Ma'am.
Haben Sie Pique gespielt?	Did you play the spade?
Ja, mein Herr.	Yes, Sir.
Dann haben Sie Farbe verläugnet.	Then you have revoked.
Wie viel Trümpfe hatten Sie?	How many trumps had you?
Ich hatte die Königin mit fünf Trümpfen.	I had the queen and five trumps.

Ich hatte mit dem Buben vier Trümpfe.	I had with the knave four trumps.
Ich hatte mit dem Aß fünf Trümpfe.	I had four trumps besides the ace.
Sie hatten sehr hohe Karten.	You had very high cards.
Ich hatte sehr schlechte Karten.	I had very bad cards.
Was muß ich anlegen?	How many must I mark?
Ich hatte selbst vier Honneurs in der Hand.	I had four honors in my own hand.
Sie haben zwei Stiche und vier Honneurs verloren.	They have lost two by tricks and four by honors.
Ich hatte Treff-Aß und den Buben.	I had the ace of clubs and the knave.
Sie haben drei Stiche und zwei Honneurs gewonnen.	You have won three by tricks and two by honors.
Wir haben das Spiel verloren.	We have lost the game.
Was haben Sie gewonnen?	What have you won?
Einen simpeln gegen einen simpeln von Ihnen, einen doppelten und den Robber.	A single to your single, a double and the rubber.

In der Schule.	IN SCHOOL.
Ich kann nicht mit dieser Feder schreiben.	I cannot write with this pen.
Haben Sie die Güte mir eine Feder zu schneiden.	Have the kindness to make me a pen.
Ich schnitt Ihnen diesen Morgen eine.	I made you one this morning.
Sie taugt nicht.	It is good for nothing.
Die Tinte ist zu dick, sie fließt nicht.	The ink is too thick, it does not run.
Ich bin mit meiner Aufgabe beinahe fertig.	I have almost done my exercise.
Ich habe eine Seite geschrieben.	I have written a page.

Ich muß meine Aufgabe schreiben.	I must write my exercise.
Ich werde meine Aufgabe in weniger als zehn Minuten fertig haben.	I shall have my exercise ready in less than ten minutes.
Schreiben Sie sie gut und ohne Fehler.	Write it well and without faults.
Ich will mich in Acht nehmen, keinen zu machen.	I will take care not to make any.
Sehr wohl; ich sehe, daß Sie fleißig sind.	Very good, *or* very well, I see that you are diligent.
Was lernest du in der Schule?	What do you learn at school?
Ich lerne die teutsche und französische Sprache.	I learn the German and French languages.
Was denken Sie von der deutschen Sprache?	What do you think of the German language?
Ich denke, daß sie eine sehr nützliche und schöne Sprache ist; aber ich denke, sie ist sehr schwer.	I think that it is a very useful and beautiful language; but I think it is very difficult.
Der Anfang ist es immer.	The beginning is always so.
Haben Sie Ihre Lection gelernt?	Have you learnt your lesson?
Sie lesen recht gut.	You read very well.
Legen Sie die Bücher auf den Tisch.	Put the books upon the table.
Haben Sie die Zeitwörter gelernt?	Have you learnt the verbs?
Nein, noch nicht, sie sind sehr schwer zu lernen.	No, not yet, they are very difficult to learn.
Sind Sie nicht faul?	Are you not idle?
Nein, ich bin heute sehr fleißig.	No, I am very diligent today.
Ich habe mein Buch verloren, ich kann es nicht finden.	I have lost my book, I cannot find it.

Wo legten Sie es hin?	Where did you put it?
Ich legte es auf den Tisch.	I put it upon the table.
Vielleicht hat jemand es für das seinige genommen.	Perhaps some one has taken it for his own.
Fragen Sie, ob es nicht jemand von Ihren Cameraden hat.	Ask if one of your companions has not got it.
Hier ist es.	Here it is.
Warum nehmen Sie nicht Ihr eigenes?	Why do you not take your own?
Ich dachte, er hätte seines nicht nöthig.	I thought he did not want his.
Sie sprechen ohne Kenntniß.	You speak without knowing.
Ich habe mein Exercitium fertig.	I have my exercise ready.
Ich werde meine Aufgabe lernen.	I shall learn my problem.
Machen Sie nicht so viel Geräusch, ich kann meine Lection nicht lernen.	Do not make so much noise, I cannot learn my lesson.
Er bereuet seine Faulheit.	He repents his idleness.
Er weiß seine Lection.	He knows his lesson.
Sie sind zuweilen sehr faul.	You are sometimes very idle.
Ja, aber ich bin das nicht immer.	Yes, but I am not always so.
Leihen Sie mir einen Bogen Papier.	Lend me a sheet of paper.
Ich möchte gern einen Brief schreiben.	I wish to write a letter.
Welche Art Papier wollen Sie haben?	What kind of paper will you have?
Schreibpapier.	Writing-paper.
Brauchen Sie eine Feder? Ich habe eine, die sehr gut ist.	Do you want a pen? I have one which is very good.
Ich danke Ihnen, ich bin damit versehen.	I thank you, I am provided with pens.
Sie schreiben immer schlechter.	You write worse and worse.

Sie geben sich jetzt weniger Mühe. — You take less pains now.

Bewegen Sie den Tisch nicht. — Do not shake the table.

Ich that es nicht mit Vorsatz. — I did not do it on purpose.

Leihen Sie mir Ihren Schiefer. — Lend me your slate.

Was ist aus dem Ihrigen geworden? — What has become of yours?

Er ist zerbrochen. — It is broken, *or* in pieces.

Fordern Sie einen andern. — Ask for another.

Ich wage es nicht, mein Lehrer würde schelten. — I dare not, my teacher would scold.

Gehen Sie und hohlen Sie meinen, aber machen Sie geschwind, ich werde ihn bald gebrauchen. — Go and fetch mine, but make haste, I shall soon want it.

Ich werde mein Exercitium in weniger als zehn Minuten fertig haben. — I shall have done my exercise in less than ten minutes.

Um sich in ein Packetboot einzuschiffen.
TO EMBARK IN A PACKET-BOAT.

Können Sie mir wohl sagen, ob im Hafen ein Packetboot nach Frankreich segelfertig liegt? — Can you tell me whether there is a packet in the harbour ready to sail for France?

Ich glaube es sind zwei da. — I believe there are two.

Hier ist ein Matrose, von dem, das zuerst abgehet. — Here is one of the crew of that which is to sail first.

Mein Freund, wo ist Euer Capitain? — My good man, where is your captain?

Da kommt er auf uns zu. — There he is coming towards us

Guten Tag, Herr Capitain; wann denken Sie unter Segel zu gehen? — Good morning, captain, when do you expect to sail?

Ich werde morgen mit der ersten Fluth abgehen, wenn der Wind gut ist.

I shall go by the first tide to-morrow, if the wind is favorable.

Warum gehen Sie nicht schon mit der heutigen Fluth ab?

Why do you not go to-day by the next tide?

Ich glaube, daß wir ein Gewitter bekommen werden.

I think we shall have a storm.

Der Wind erhebt sich stark.

The wind gets much higher.

Welch schrecklicher Sturm!

What a dreadful storm!

Ist es noch immer Gegenwind?

Does the contrary wind still continue?

Zu welcher Stunde werden Sie morgen unter Segel gehen?

At what o'clock shall you sail to-morrow?

Zu welcher Stunde muß ich bereit seyn?

At what o'clock must I be ready?

Sie brauchen mir nur Ihre Wohnung anzugeben, ich werde Sie dann durch einen meiner Matrosen benachrichtigen lassen.

You have only to tell me where you lodge, and one of my sailors shall come and inform you, *or* give you notice.

Beim Einschiffen, und bei einer Seereise.

ON EMBARKING, AND A VOYAGE AT SEA.

Wann wird man sich einschiffen müssen?

When must we go on board?

Meine Herren, man wird unter Segel gehen, und wartet nur auf Sie.

Gentlemen, they are going to sail, and are only waiting for you.

Wir sind bereit; nehmt diese beiden Mantelsäcke.

We are ready, take these two portmanteaus.

Wie viel muß man für die Ueberfahrt zahlen?

How much must we pay for the passage?

Zehn Schillinge und sechs Pence für die Person.

Ten *shillings* and sixpence each.

Neun Mark.
Steigen Sie in die Schaluppe, meine Herren; geben Sie Acht das Sie sich nicht beschädigen.
Wie lange wird unsre Wasserfahrt dauern, wenn wir günstiges Wetter haben?
Nicht mehr als drei Stunden.
Die See scheint mir sehr unruhig.
Es ist nichts, es ist keine Gefahr.
Es ist nichts zu fürchten.
Die See geht aber sehr hoch.
Das Schwanken des Schiffes macht mir übel.
Legen Sie sich, es wird Ihnem wohl thun.

Nine marks.
Get, or step into the boat, gentlemen, and take care not to hurt yourselves.
How long shall we be on our passage, if we have favorable weather?
Not more than three hours.
The sea seems to me to be very rough.
That is nothing; there is no danger.
There is nothing to fear.
But the sea is very high.
The rolling of the ship makes me ill.
Lie down, it will do you good.

Gespräch in einem Schiffe.

CONVERSATION ON BOARD A SHIP.

Wie lange werden wir auf dem Meere seyn?
Ich kann es Ihnen nicht sagen, weil in dieser Jahreszeit der Wind nicht beständig ist.
Bis jetzt haben wir günstigen Wind, und unser Schiff segelt gut.
Ich fürchte, wir werden ein Gewitter bekommen; der Himmel ist im Westen sehr trübe.

How long shall we be at sea?
I cannot tell you; because in this season the wind is not constant.
So far the wind is very favorable, and the ship goes well.
I fear we shall have a storm; the sky is very cloudy in the west.

Glauben Sie, daß Gefahr vorhanden sey?
Do you think there is any danger?

Fürchten Sie sich nicht; es hat keine Gefahr.
Do not be afraid, there is no danger.

Um welche Zeit werden wir ankommen?
At what time shall we arrive?

Ich habe sehr starkes Kopfweh; der Geruch des Theers macht mir übel.
I have a very bad headache; the smell of the tar makes me ill.

Riechen Sie ein wenig an Cölnisches Wasser, das wird Ihnen gut thun.
Smell a little *Eau-de-Cologne*: it will do you good.

Ich habe eine große Neigung zum Erbrechen.
I have a great inclination to be sick; *or* to sickness.

Ich leide gewaltig; ich werde mich erbrechen; geben Sie mir das Becken.
I suffer exceedingly; I shall be sick; give me the basin.

Seyn Sie so gütig, das Fenster oder die Fenster zu öffnen.
Be so kind as to open the window, *or* windows.

Werden wir das Fahrzeug verlassen, und in eine Schaluppe steigen müssen?
Shall we be obliged to leave the ship and go into the boat?

Ja, man muß in die Schaluppe steigen.
Yes, you must step into the boat.

Ich nehme bloß mein Nachtzeug mit.
I shall only take my night clothes with me.

Wird man von den Zollbeamten beim Landen visitirt?
Shall we be visited by the custom-house officers?

Besuch der Zollbeamten.

VISIT OF THE CUSTOM-HOUSE OFFICERS.

Meine Herren, hier sind die Zollbeamten.
Gentlemen, here are the custom-house officers.

Haben Sie nichts bei sich, was gegen die Gesetze ist?

Have you nothing with **you** that is illegal?

Nein, ich habe keine Contrebante, oder ich habe nichts Verbotenes.

No, I have no contraband goods, *or* I have nothing that is prohibited.

Meine Herren, Ihre Felleisen, Mantelsäcke, Koffer und Packete, müssen nach dem Zollhause gebracht werde.

Gentlemen, you must have your trunks, portmanteaus, boxes and parcels, taken to the custom-house.

Ich habe nur wenige Sachen, welche Accise geben, und ich will sie anzeigen.

I have only a few things which pay duty, and I will show them.

Wie viel habe ich für dieses zu bezahlen?

How much have I to pay for this?

Sie haben fünf Schillinge zu bezahlen.

You have five shillings to pay.

Ich bin sehr ermüdet von der Seereise, und wünschte mich im Gasthofe auszuruhen.

I am very much fatigued from the sea voyage, and could wish to rest myself at the inn.

Geben Sie mir Ihre Schlüssel, und Sie können sich hinbegeben, wohin es Ihnen beliebt.

Give me your keys, and you can then go where you please.

Hier sind sie. Haben Sie die Güte, etwas schnell zu machen, denn ich bin sehr in Eile.

Here they are. Have the goodness to be a little quick, for I am in a great hurry.

Ein Träger wird meinen Koffer und Sachen nach dem Zollhause bringen, und ich werde ihm folgen.

A porter will carry my trunk and things to the custom-house, and I will follow him.

Nach Belieben, *or* Wie Ihnen gefällig ist.

As you please, *or* as you **like**.

Haben Sie die Güte, mit Vorsicht zu visitiren, es sind viel zerbrechliche Sachen darin.	Have the kindness to be careful in examining, for there are many things that are easily broken.

Um eine Wohnung zu miethen.

ON HIRING A LODGING.

Haben Sie Zimmer zu vermiethen? Ich brauche ein Logis, *or,* Ich bedarf einer Wohnung.	Have you any rooms to let? I want a lodging, *or* an apartment.
Oh ja, ich habe deren im ersten, zweiten und im dritten Stock, nach der Straße.	Yes, Sir, I have, on the first, second, and third story, next to the street.
Wollen Sie sie möblirt oder nicht möblirt haben?	Will you have them furnished *or* unfurnished?
Ich muß möblirte Zimmer haben.	I must have furnished rooms.
Ich muß zwei Schlafzimmer haben, nebst einer Wohnstube und einer Küche.	I must have two bed-rooms, with a parlour and kitchen.
Mit dem allen kann ich Sie versehen. Wollen Sie gefälligst hereinkommen?	I can accommodate you with them all. Will you please to walk in?
Meine Gemahlin muß ihre Kammerfrau in ihrer Nähe haben.	My wife must have her chamber-maid near her.
Ich habe Zimmer, neben welchen sich ein kleines für die Kammerfrau befindet.	I have apartments, where there is a small room for the lady's-maid.
Lassen Sie mich sie sehen.	Let me see them.
Dies ist sehr bequem für uns.	This is very convenient for us.

Sehen Sie, die Treppe ist hell und bequem.	Look, Sir, the stair-case is light and convenient.
Wie viele Betten sind da?	How many beds are there?
Vier sehr gute.	Four very good ones.
Ich will sehen, ob das Bett gut ist, denn das ist eine Hauptsache.	I will see whether the bed is good, for that is the principal thing.
Wenn ich ein gutes Bett habe, so mache ich mir nicht viel aus dem Uebrigen.	If I have a good bed, I do not care much about the rest.
Ich denke das Bett ist gut. Nun möchte ich nur noch den Preis wissen.	I think the bed is good. Now I only wish to know what is the price.
Was verlangen Sie für die drei Zimmer und die Küche?	What do you ask for the three rooms and the kitchen?
Vierhundert Franken monatlich.	Four hundred francs a month.
Ich gebe Ihnen dreihundert und fünfzig dafür.	I will give you three hundred and fifty for them.
Es ist das Aeußerste und gewiß sehr billig.	It is the lowest, and certainly very cheap.
Wie viel verlangen Sie die Woche dafür?	How much do you ask for it a week?
Hundert und zwanzig Franken wöchentlich.	A hundred and twenty francs a week.
Wie viel nehmen Sie für Mittag- und Abendessen?	How much do you ask for dinner and supper?
Zwei Mark für die Person für jede Mahlzeit, das Frühstück wird besonders bezahlt.	Two marks a head for each meal, besides breakfast.
Das ist zu theuer. Ich will lieber nach der Karte speisen.	That is too dear. I had rather be served by the bill of fare *or* dish.

Wie Ihnen gefällig ist.	As you please, Sir.
Lassen Sie mich das Zimmer sehen, welches Sie für mich bestimmen.	Let me see the room which you intend for me.
Dieses ist es. Es ist sehr schön und bequem.	This is it., Sir, it is very pretty and convenient.
Wann denken Sie Ihre Wohnung zu beziehen?	When do you intend to take possession.
Ich beabsichtige diese Nacht hier zu schlafen.	I intend to sleep here to-night.
Sehr wohl, Sie können kommen, so bald Sie wollen.	Very well, Sir, you can come as soon as you like, *or* please.

SENTENCES ILLUSTRATING THE APPLICATION OF PARTICULAR WORDS.

An, zu, in, bei, nach, von, u. s. w.	AT, TO, IN, BY, WITH, NEAR, &c.
Man ist am Hause, ehe man im Hause ist.	A person is at the house, before he is in it.
Mein Hund heult an der Thüre.	My dog howls at the door or gate.
Ich bin in London geboren.	I was born in London.
Ich werde zu Hause seyn.	I shall be at home.
Mein Vater verschaffte mir eine Wohnung im Hause des Hrn. Read.	My father procured me a lodging at Mr. Read's.
Ich gehe nach London.	I am going to London.
Er spricht zu (mit) Leuten von Verstand.	He speaks to (*with*) men of understanding.
Er wohnt bei mir, dir, u. s. w., er war bei Ihnen.	He lives with me, thee, &c,, he was at your house.

Um wie viel Uhr essen Sie? At what hour do you dine?
Ich habe kein Geld bei mir I have no money by me.
Er wird von jedermann geliebt. He is loved by every body.
Dies Gemälde ist von Raphael. This painting is by Raphael.
Es ist bei Herr Balne gedruckt. It was printed by Mr. Balne.
Ich kehrte über Amsterdam zu= I came home *or* returned by
rück. Amsterdam.
Er starb durch das Schwert. He died by the sword.
Wir verkaufen im Großen, aber We sell by wholesale, but
nicht im Einzelnen. not by retail.
Er nahm es mit Gewalt. He took it by force.
Er ward auf des Königs Befehl He was beheaded by the
enthauptet. king's order.
Sie reisen zu Lande oder zu See. They travel by land or by
sea.
Er ist über Frankreich nach Eng= He has travelled by France
land gereiset. to England.

So, als, wie.   AS, LIKE, &c.

Es ist so breit als lang. It is as broad as long.
Ich bin so wohl hier als dort. I am as well here as there.
Geben Sie mir so wenig als Sie Give me as little as you
wollen. please.
Das Wasser ist so hell als That water is as clear as
Kristall. crystal.
Ich weiß, daß Sie so gut sind I know that you are as good
als ich. as I.
Ich bin nicht so gelehrt als Sie. I am not so learned as you.
Ich lebe wie ich lebte, ich denke I live as I did, I think as I
wie ich dachte. did.
Die Welt wird weder handeln The world will neither act
noch denken wie ich. nor think as I do.
Thun Sie wie ich Ihnen sage, Do as I tell you, *or* as I
or befehle. order you.

Als, wie.

Er handelt als ein rechtschaffner Mann.
Er hielt sich wie ein Mann.

Er handelt wie ein Vater gegen mich.
Ich weiß, daß er reicher ist als ich.
Sie brüllten wie die Löwen.
Monarchie ist besser als Anarchie.

Ich kann nicht sagen, wie ich Sie liebe.
Ich kann nicht sagen, wie sehr mich dieses betrübt.

Außer, aber, nur, u. s. w.

Wir waren alle dort, außer euch.
Er ist ein guter Vater, aber etwas zu nachsichtig.
Er hatte nur einen Freund.
Sie thaten nichts als klagen.

Ich habe es nicht nur gesehen, sondern auch gehöret.
Ich zweifle nicht, daß Sie mein Freund sind.
Sie sind alle fleißig, ausgenommen Sie.
Sie sind nicht meine Freunde, sondern meine Feinde.

LIKE, THAN, HOW.

He acts *like* or *as* an honest man.
He behaved himself like a man.
He acted like a father towards me.
I know that he is richer than I.
They roared like lions.
Monarchy is better than anarchy.
I cannot say how much I love you.
I cannot say how much this afflicts me.

EXCEPT, BUT, &c.

We were all there except, *or* but you.
He is a good father, but rather too indulgent.
He had but one friend.
They did nothing but complain.
I have not only seen it, but have also heard it.
I do not doubt but, *or* that you are my friend.
They are all diligent, but *or* except you.
They are not my friends, but my enemies.

PROVERBS, IDIOMS, &c.

Die Zeit bringt Rath.
Time brings counsel.

Wissenschaft herrscht immer über Unwissenheit.
Knowledge always predominates over ignorance.

Thorheit und Narrheit ist der Weisheit und Klugheit entgegen gesetzt.
Stupidity and folly are the opposites of wisdom and prudence.

Die Weisheit will, daß ich mein Leben nicht ohne Noth in Gefahr setze.
Wisdom requires that I should not put my life in danger without necessity.

Nichts wissen ist keine Schande, wohl aber nichts lernen wollen.
Ignorance is no disgrace, but not wishing to learn is a disgrace.

Selten wird das Treffliche gefunden, seltener geschätzt.
The excellent is seldom found, and seldomer valued.

Die Kunst ist lang, das Leben kurz, das Urtheil schwierig, die Gelegenheit flüchtig.
Art is long, life is short, judgment difficult, opportunity fleeting.

Niemand ist im Universum so sehr allein als ein Gottesläugner.
No one is so much alone in the world as an atheist.

Man wird oft lästig, wenn man zu höflich seyn will.
A person often becomes troublesome, by wishing to be too polite.

Wer die wahre christliche Liebe im Herzen trägt, wird es durch sein äußeres Betragen seinem Nächsten zeigen.
Whoever has true Christian charity in the heart, will shew it by his outward conduct to his neighbour.

Das schwere Herz wird nicht durch Worte leicht.
A heavy heart is not made light by words.

Der brave Mann denkt an sich selbst zuletzt.

Ertragen muß man, was der Himmel sendet.

Die Gerichte Gottes sind gerecht.

Die Eigenliebe ist der größte von allen Schmeichlern.

Was die dunkle Nacht gesponnen soll frei und fröhlich an das Licht der Sonnen.

Wer gar zu viel bedenkt, wird wenig leisten.

Der fürchtet keine Götter, der keines Menschen schont.

Ein furchtbar wüthend Schreckniß ist der Krieg, die Heerde schlägt er und den Hirten.

Nichts ist wahrer, als der Ausspruch von Heinrich dem Vierten: „Daß man mehr Fliegen in einem Löffel voll Honig fangen kann, als in einem Oxhoft voll Essig."

Etwas fürchten und hoffen und sorgen muß der Mensch für den kommenden Morgen, daß er die Schwere des Daseyns ertrage.

An honest man thinks of himself last.

We must endure what heaven decrees.

The judgments of God are just.

Self love is the greatest of all flatterers.

The web that's spun at night, looks fair and perfect in the morning's light.

He who reflects too much, will do but little.

He has no fear for the gods, who has no compassion for men

War is a frightful raging monster, which slays alike the shepherd and the sheep.

Nothing is truer than the saying of Henry the Fourth; "That more flies are caught with à spoonful of honey, than with a hogshead of vinegar!"

Man must fear, and hope and care something for the coming morrow that he may bear the burden of existence.

Einladungsbriefe, Karten, Billets, u. s. w.

Einladungsbriefe.

Geehrter Herr!

Nächsten Dienstag haben wir eine ausgewählte musikalische Gesellschaft. Wir würden uns sehr geschmeichelt fühlen, wollten Sie uns die mächtige Hülfe Ihres herrlichen Talents zu Theil werden lassen. Bitte, täuschen Sie unsere Hoffnung nicht.

Ihr Sie schätzender,

S. E. R.

Freitag Abend.

Antwort.

Das Vergnügen, verehrter Freund, einen Abend in der angenehmen Gesellschaft zuzubringen, die ich immer in Ihrem Hause finde, veranlaßt mich, Ihre gütige Einladung bereitwillig anzunehmen, und wenn ich mich auf irgend eine Weise nützlich machen kann, so haben Sie nur zu befehlen.

Ihr Ergebener,

J. P. R.

Sonnabend Morgen.

LETTERS OF INVITATION, CARDS, NOTES, &c.

A LETTER OF INVITATION.

My dear Sir,

On Tuesday next we have a select musical party. We shall feel ourselves exceedingly flattered, if you will favor us with the powerful assistance of your splendid talents. I trust you will not disappoint us.

I am, my dear Sir,
Yours very truly,
G. C. R.

Friday Evening.

ANSWER.

The pleasure, my dear friend, of spending an Evening in the agreeable society I always meet at your house, prompts me to accept your kind invitation ; and, if I can in any way render myself useful, you have only to command,

Yours very truly,
J. P. S.

Saturday Morning.

Einladungs-Billet.

Madame E. empfiehlt sich Herrn N. bestens, und bittet ihn, ihr die Ehre zu erzeigen, nächsten Donnerstag um 5 Uhr bei ihr zu Mittag zu speisen. Herr N. wird das Vergnügen haben, die Person zu finden, deren Bekanntschaft er zu machen wünscht.

Antwort.

Ich kann übermorgen nicht das Vergnügen haben, mit Ihnen zu Mittage zu speisen, weil mein Vater einige Personen zum Mittagessen hat, und ich da bleiben muß, um ihnen Gesellschaft zu leisten; aber ich werde Sie morgen zwischen 11 und 12 Uhr besuchen Adieu.

Einladungs-Billet.

Herr und Madame R. bitten sich von Herrn und Madame P. die Ehre aus, morgen Abend bei ihnen zuzubringen zum Thee und Abendessen *or* Abendbrob (*or* bitten sich für Morgen die Ehre ihres Besuchs zum Thee und Abendbbrob aus).

Antwort.

Herr und Frau (*or* Madame) P. senden Herrn und Madame R. ihre Empfehlung, und ihre gütige Einladung annehmend, werden das Vergnügen haben, aufzuwarten.

A NOTE OF INVITATION.

Mrs. C. presents her best compliments to Mr. N., and requests the honor of his company to dinner on Thursday next, at five o'clock. Mr. N. will have the pleasure of meeting the person with whom he wishes to form an acquaintance.

ANSWER.

I cannot have the pleasure of dining with you to-morrow, because my father will have some persons to dine with him, and I must stay to keep them company; but I will come and see you to-morrow between eleven and twelve. Adieu.

A NOTE OF INVITATION.

Mr. and Mrs. R. have the honor to present their compliments to Mr. and Mrs. P. and request the favor of their company to-morrow evening to tea and supper.

ANSWER.

Mr. and Mrs. P. present their compliments to Mr. and Mrs. R. and will have much pleasure in accepting their kind invitation for to-morrow evening.

Einladungs-Billet.

Madame A. hat die Ehre, Herrn R. freundlich zu grüßen, und ihn zu bitten, morgen den Abend bei ihr zuzubringen. Es wird Musik gemacht.

Entschuldigungs-Billet.

Herr. R. bittet Mad. A. ihn zu entschuldigen, daß er nicht von ihrer angenehmen Einladung Gebrauch machen kann, da er schon seit drei Tagen durch Unpäßlichkeit zu Hause gehalten wird. Unterdessen hat er die Ehre sich ihr mit der ausgezeichnetsten Achtung zu empfehlen.

Einladungs-Karte.

Herr A. empfiehlt sich Fräulein B. gehorsamst, und bittet um die Ehre, sie in die morgen statt habende Abendgesellschaft führen zu dürfen.

Antwort.

Fräulein B. dankt Herrn A. für seine Artigkeit, und bedauert, daß sie sein Anerbieten nicht annehmen kann, weil sie schon engagirt ist.

Einladungs-Karte.

Fräulein N. empfiehlt sich höflich Lady E., und bittet um die Ehre ihrer Gesellschaft für diesen Abend zum Thee und Kartenspiel.

Antwort.

Lady E. dankt Fräulein N. für ihre gütige Einladung, wovon sie die Ehre haben wird Gebrauch zu machen.

A NOTE OF INVITATION.

Mrs. A. has the honor to present her compliments to Mr. R. and requests the pleasure of his company to-morrow evening.

There will be music.

A NOTE OF APOLOGY.

Mr. R. requests Mrs. A. will excuse him for not being able to accept her kind invitation, having been confined at home from indisposition for these three days past. In the mean time he has the honor of presenting her his best respects.

A CARD OF INVITATION.

Mr. A. presents his respectful compliments to Miss B., and requests the honor of her hand at the assembly to-morrow evening.

ANSWER.

Miss B. thanks Mr. A. for his politeness, and is sorry that she cannot accept his offer, being already engaged.

AN INVITATION CARD.

Miss N.——'s respectful compliments to Lady E., and begs the honor of her company this evening to tea and cards.

ANSWER.

Lady E. thanks Miss N. for her kind invitation, which she will have the honor to accept.

EXPLANATIONS RESPECTING THE GERMAN COINAGE.

About the year 1750, in consequence of the coinage in Germany being much debased, the princes of most of the German States agreed to have one fixed standard of value for their different coins; for which purpose a Convention or agreement was signed; except for Hamburgh, Mecklenburgh, Lübeck, Bremen, Hanover, the Danish provinces of Germany, Oldenburg, and a few other places which retained their own standard unchanged. The coin which was issued according to this convention was, and is, called Conventions Fuss[*].

The standard[†] according to the convention is, that from one mark Cöln (Cologne) which equals 7 oz. 10 dwt. 8 grs. English, of fine silver, there should be coined 20 florins, or gulden, which is called the 20 Florin, or 20 Gulden Fuss. (Gulden is often called Guilder by the English.) The southern states of Germany reckon by florins, or gulden of 60 kreutzers each. The northern states reckon by thalers, or, as we call them, dollars of 1½ gulden each or 30 groschen.

If we reckon an ounce of fine silver to be worth 5s. English, the Cöln mark will be worth about 40s. sterling. Hence 1 gulden, or florin, is worth about 2s.; and 1½ gulden, which equals 1 dollar, convention money, is worth about 3s. sterling English, *more* or *less*, according to the course of exchange.

---

[*] Observe. Fuß, literally *foot*, means *rate*, or *standard*.

[†] According to the old standard, viz., the 17 gulden fuss, which is only used in Mecklenburgh, Denmark, Hamburgh, and Lübeck, they only made 17 gulden from 1, Cöln mark of fine silver.

AUSTRIA, and all the southern states, as well as all the spiritual electorates on the Rhine (Treves, Mayence, aud Cologne) used to coin 2 gulden pieces, or species-thaler, 1 gulden, and ½ gulden, or 30 kreutzer pieces; also 20, 15, 10, and 5 kreutzer pieces (Stücke, agreeably to the convention; out it is only in Austria that these coins pass for their nominal value;—in all the other southern states they have adopted the 24 gulden fuss, that is to say, they make 24 gulden instead of 20 gulden, from 1 mark of fine silver, which is commonly called Rhenish money. This is done for the convenience of trade with Holland, the Dutch gulden being equal to about 1 gulden Rhenish, or 1s. 8d. sterling English. Six gulden Rhenish are equal to five gulden convention money. The 20 kreutzer piece passes in Austria for 20 kreutzer; but in all those states where they have adopted the 24 gulden fuss, it passes for 24 kreutzers.

Thus,

	Florin or gulden.	Kreutzers.		s.	d.	
1 Gulden,* Convention Money	= 1	12 Rhenish,		2	0	English.
or 1 guld. or 60 krs. .... do....	= 0	72 .... do.	=	2	0	do.
30 Kreutzers .... do....	= 0	36 .... do.	=	1	0	do.
20........ do............. do....	= 0	24 .... do.	=	0	8	do.
15........ do............. do....	= 0	18 .... do.	=	0	6	do.
10........ do............. do....	= 0	12 .... do.	=	0	4	do.
5........ do............. do....	= 0	6 .... do.	=	0	2	do.
1........ do.......... Rhenish Money............			=	0	0½	do.

Subsequently, some of the states that signed the Convention, have deviated from its regulations, and discontinued coining at the 20 gulden rate. Prussia now coins at the 21 gulden fuss, that is to say, they make 21 gulden from 1 mark Cöln fine silver. Hence 105 dollars Prussian money = 100 dollars Convention money. The money of Hessia is about ½ per cent. inferior to that of Prussia.

* Observe. The gulden varies in value according to the course of exchange

Those States that excluded themselves from the Convention, retained their own standard, viz., Denmark (for its German provinces). Hamburgh and Lubeck coin 17 gulden, or 34 marks, from 1 mark Cologne of silver. Mecklenburgh and Hanover coined about 18 gulden from the Cöln mark.

The circulating medium of Hanover was called Cassengeld, but about the year 1852, it was discontinued, and Convention money was substituted in its stead; lately, however, the latter has also been discontinued, and the Prussian, or 21 gulden fuss is now adopted.

Bremen is the only place in Germany where gold can be considered as a legal tender, for in all other parts the gold coins are constantly varying in value, and are considered as merchandise; silver coins being the only legal tender. The five-dollar piece, in gold, is valued at 72 Peter-männchen per dollar.

Observe, that with regard to the larger coins of the Convention money, such as the Species-thalers, or 2 gulden pieces, at 32 Groschen each Thaler, as well as the 1 gulden and ½ gulden pieces, there are very few in circulation; and those which are, being objects of trade among the bankers, bear a premium, against the minor ones, of from ¼ to 1¾ per cent.

The smaller coins of the Convention money being more alloyed, and generally more worn than the larger coins, their value is somewhat depressed, for instance, 100 dolls. Convention money ought to be equal to 105 dolls. Prussian money, whereas in general 100 dolls. Convention money, of the smaller coins, will only buy from 102 to 103 dolls. Prussian money.

Travellers, in the north of Germany, and on the Rhine, will find it most advantageous to carry with them Prussian paper-notes, and some silver, or five-dollar pieces in gold, commonly called Louis d'or, or Friedrichs d'or. The five dollar pieces even pass at the Prussian post-offices for 5¾ dollars, Prussian money. In the southern states, Nassau, Baden, Wirtemberg, and Bavaria, as well as at Frankfurt on the Maine, Kronen thaler (crown dollars), and 20, 10, and 5 kreutzer pieces are most advantageous. The Kronen thaler passes for 2 gulden, 42 kreutzers Rhenish money, and the 20 kreutzer for 24 kreutzer, as previously stated.

Having laid it down as a general principle, that 1 mark Cologne = 40 shillings English, we furnish the following tables; observing that there are besides, not only 5 and 10 dollar pieces current in Germany, but also ducats and double ducats; the five-dollar piece being worth about 16s. 6d., and the ducat from 8s. 11d. to 9s. 3d. English.

₊ *For the preceding particulars respecting the German coins, the Author has to acknowledge his obligations to a friend from Dresden.*

GERMAN MONEYS.

BERLIN, COLOGNE, and all the PRUSSIAN DOMINIONS, reckon by *dollars* at 30 *silver groschen.*

Gold Coins.

	Dol. s.gr.*	Dol. g.gr.*	£ s. d.
1 Doppelter Friedrichs d'or.. =	11 10 =	11 8 =	1 12 10
1 Friedrichs d'or*............. =	5 20 =	5 16 =	0 16 5
1 Halber Friedrichs d'or ...... =	2 25 =	2 20 =	0 8 2½

* Obs. 1.—Although the *Friedrichs d'or* was originally issued at 5 dollars, it is now valued at 5 dollars, 20 *s. gr.* (Obs. *s. gr.* stands for *silber groschen.*)

2.—*One pound* English=6⅔ dollars, but it varies according to the course of exchange from 6 *thalers*, 23 *s. gr.* to 6 *thal.* 26 *s gr.*

3.—Besides the above coins, there are 1, 2, 5, and 50 *dollar notes* in circulation.

4.—*One dollar* Prussian money is exchange for 1 *gulden*, 45 *kreutzers* Rhenish, or 105 *kreutzers*, that is nearly 3*s*. English.

GERMAN MONEYS.

SILVER COINS.

	s. g.	£	s.	d.	
1 Rix dollar, or reichsthaler .... =	30 =	0	2	$10\frac{1}{2}$	to 3s.
1 Halb thaler, *or* $\frac{1}{2}$ dollar .... =	15 =	0	1	$5\frac{1}{4}$	
1 En Drittel thaler, *or* $\frac{1}{3}$ dollar .... =	10 =	0	1	0	nearly
1 En Viertel thaler, *or* $\frac{1}{4}$ dollar .... =	$7\frac{1}{2}$ =	0	0	$8\frac{3}{4}$	....do.
1 Sechstel thaler, *or* $\frac{1}{6}$ dollar .... =	5 =	0	0	6	....do.
1 Zwölftel thaler, *or,* $\frac{1}{12}$ dollar .... =	$2\frac{1}{2}$ =	0	0	3	....do.

COPPER AND SILVER.

	s.gr.	£	s.	d.
1 Silber groschen (*Contracted.* s. gr.) ...... =	1 =	0	0	$1\frac{1}{4}$
1 Halb silber groschen ...... = 6 pfennige =	$\frac{1}{2}$ =	0	0	$0\frac{1}{2}$

COPPER.

		s qr.	£	s.	d.	
1 Sechs pfennig .... = $\frac{1}{60}$ of a dollar. =	$\frac{1}{2}$ =	0	0	$0\frac{3}{4}$	nearly
1 Vier pfennig .... = $\frac{1}{90}$ ......do. ... =	$\frac{1}{3}$ =	0	0	$0\frac{1}{2}$	
1 Drei pfennig .... = $\frac{1}{120}$......do. ... =	$\frac{1}{4}$ =	0	0	$0\frac{3}{10}$	
1 Zwei pfennig .... = $\frac{1}{180}$......do. ... =	$\frac{1}{6}$ =	0	0	$0\frac{1}{4}$	
1 Pfennig .... = $\frac{1}{360}$......do. ... =	$\frac{1}{12}$ =	0	0	$0\frac{1}{10}$	

BAVARIA, WIRTEMBERG, BADEN and NASSAU, reckon by *Gulden* or *florins,* at 60 *kreutzers* each, *Rhenish.*

GOLD COINS.

	Rhenish, or 24 guld. fuss.	Convention, or 20 guld. fuss.	£	s.	d.
1 Carolin (also $\frac{1}{2}$ and $\frac{1}{4}$) .... =	11 =	...... $9\frac{1}{2}$ =	.. 0	18	$4\frac{1}{2}$
1 Doppelter Max d'or........ =	$14\frac{2}{3}$=	...... $12\frac{2}{3}$ =	.. 1	7	3
1 Max d'or .... =	$7\frac{1}{3}$=	...... $6\frac{1}{3}$ =	.. 0	13	$7\frac{1}{2}$
1 Ducaten, or ducat......... =	$5\frac{1}{3}$=	...... $4\frac{2}{3}$ =	.. 0	9	4

SILVER COINS.

	Rhenish flor. krs.	Convention flor.	£	s.	d.
1 Speciesthaler, *or* dollar .... =	2 24 =	2 ...... =	0	4	1
1 Gulden, or $\frac{1}{2}$ speciesthaler ...... =	1 12 =	1 Florin =	0	2	$0\frac{1}{2}$
1 Halber gulden, *or* $\frac{1}{2}$ florin........ =	0 36 =	30 Krs. =	0	1	$0\frac{1}{4}$
1 Kronenthaler, *or* crown dollar .. =	2 42 =	....	0	4	$5\frac{1}{2}$
1 Halber ditto, *or* $\frac{1}{2}$ crown dollar.. =	1 21 =	....	0	2	$2\frac{3}{4}$
1 Viertel, *or* $\frac{1}{4}$ crown dollar ...... =	0 $40\frac{1}{2}$=	....	0	1	$1\frac{3}{8}$

GERMAN MONEYS

SILVER AND COPPER MIXED.

	Rhenish.	£	s.	d.
1 Kopfstück, *or* 20 kreutzer Conv. money =	24 krs. =	0	0	8
1 Halbes kopfstück, *or* 10 kreutzer stück =	12 .... =	0	0	4
1 Viertel kopfstück, *or* 5 kreutzer stück =	6 .... =	0	0	2
1 Sechs kreutzer-stück (Landmünze) .... =	6 .... =	0	0	2
1 Drei kreutzer-stück........ ditto .... =	3 .... =	0	0	1
1 Kreutzer-stück............ ditto .... =	1 .... =	0	0	$0\frac{1}{3}$
1 Pfennig (*copper coin*).................. =	$0\frac{1}{4}$ .... =	0	0	$0\frac{1}{12}$

Obs. 1. — 1 Guld. at the 20 flor. fuss, *or* Conv. money = 0 2 0
    1 Guld. ...... 24 ditto, *or* Rhenish standard = 0 1 8
    $1\frac{1}{2}$ Guld. = 1 dol. Conv. money, *or* 20 fl. rate = 0 3 0

  2.— *Speciesthaler, gulden,* and $\frac{1}{2}$ *gulden,* are no longer coined, and are seldom met with but at bankers. The dollar is worth about 4s. English, and from $\frac{1}{4}$ to $1\frac{3}{4}$ per cent. more depending on the course of exchange.

  3.—All silver coins in Bavaria are expressed according to the 20 florin fuss, or standard; but are here valued at the 24 florin fuss, or *Rhenish standard,* being $\frac{1}{5}$ more than the *Convention standard* fixed in the year 1750.

 One 20 kreutzer-stück Conv. money .... = 24 krs. Rhenish stand.
 One 10 kreutzer-stück ...... ditto .... = 12   ditto.
 Also 1 guld. Conven. money = 72 krs. and 1 guld. Rhen. = 60 krs.

HAMBURG, LÜBECK, HOLSTEIN &c.

Hamburg and Lübeck reckon in *Marks* at 16 schillings each.

Holstein, in Speciesthalers, at 3 Marks, 12 schillings, and in Marks at 16 Schillings each.

1 *Cöln Mark* of silver, by weight, is coined into 17 Gulden *or* Florins, or 34 Marks. 1 *Mark banco* = 1s. 6d. English: and 1 *Mark current* = 1s 3d. nearly. 100 *Marks banco* = 125 *Marks currency,* more or less, depending on the course of exchange.

GOLD COINS.

	Marks. bco.	Marks. cur.	£	s.	d.
2 Ducaten, *or* 2 ducats.......... =	12 =	15 ...... =	0	17	10
1 Ducaten, *or* 1 ducat .... =	6 =	$7\frac{1}{2}$ ...... =	0	8	11
1 Louis-oder Friedrichs d'or.... =	$11\frac{1}{4}$ =	$13\frac{29}{32}$ ...... =	0	16	$6\frac{1}{2}$
1 Napoleon d'or .... =	$10\frac{3}{4}$ =	$13\frac{7}{16}$ ...... =	0	15	$11\frac{1}{2}$
1 Französischer Schild-Louis d'or =	$12\frac{7}{8}$ =	$16\frac{3}{32}$ ...... =	0	19	$1\frac{1}{2}$

GERMAN MONEYS.

SILVER COINS.

	M. bco.	M. cur. schil.	schil.	£	s.	d.
1 Danish species dollar	= 3	= 3	12 = 60 =	0	4	5
1 Halb do. *or* 1 Danish reichs bank thaler	= 1	14	= 30 =	0	2	2½
1 Eindrittel species dollr	= 1	4	= 20 =	0	1	5¾
1 Zwei Mark stück, *or* 2 Mark piece			= 32 =	0	2	4¼
1 Mark Stück, *or* 1 Mark piece			= 16 =	0	1	2⅛
1 Zwei drittel Stück, *or* 1 Gulden (*Mecklenburgh*)			= 31 =	0	2	3
1 Halb Mark, *or* acht schilling stück			= 8 =	0	0	7 1/16
1 Zwölf schill. Stück, *or* 12 schill. piece			= 12 =	0	0	10¾
1 Zwanzig schilling Dansk (*Danish*)			= 10 =	0	0	8¾
1 Zehn schilling Dansk			= 5 =	0	0	4½ nearly
1 Fünf schilling Dansk			= 2½ =	0	0	2¼
1 Vier schilling stück, *or* ¼ Mark			= 4 =	0	0	3½
1 Zwei schilling stück, *or* ⅛ Mark			= 2 =	0	0	1¾
1 Schilling current			= 1 =	0	0	0⅞
1 Sechsling, *or* ½ schilling			= 0½ =	0	0	0 7/16
1 Dreiling, or dreyling			= 0¼ =	0	0	0 7/32

Obs.—The accounts at the *Bank* are kept in *Marks* and *Schillinge Banco*, an imaginary money which regulates to a certain extent, the value of the other moneys according to the rate of exchange. 13 *Marks, 8 Schillinge*, more or less, according to the exchange, equal *one pound sterling* English. Hence, 1 Mark = about 17½d. All exchanges with foreign countries, and most business transactions are settled in *Banco money*. But the circulating medium is in *currency*, which is generally somewhat higher than *banco*. The *Old species dollars*, of which there are but few, = 3 Marks banco.

DRESDEN and all SAXONY reckon in *dollars, groschen, pfenninge*. 1 dol. = 30 gros. and 1 gros. = 12 pfen.

GOLD. (*Convention Money*.)

	thal. grs.	£	s.	d.
1 Doppelter August d'or	= 11 0	= 1	13	0
1 August d'or, *or* Louis d'or	= 5 12	= 0	16	6
1 Halber Louis d'or	= 2 18	= 0	8	3
1 Doppelter ducaten	= 6 4	= 0	18	6
1 Ducaten (Dutch or Austrian)	= 3 2	= 0	9	3

Silver Coins. (*Convention Money*).

		Gute gros.		£	s.	d.
1 Species-thaler, *or* dollar	=	32	=	0	4	1
1 Reichs-thaler, *or* rix dollar	=	24	=	0	2	11½
1 Gulden, *or* halbe sp. th. *or* ⅔tel stücke..	=	16	=	0	2	0½
1 Halbe gulden, *or* ⅓tel stücke	=	8	=	0	1	0¼
1 Ein sechstel-tha. *or* vier gros. stücke ..	=	4	=	0	0	6
1 Zwölftel-tha. *or* zwei grs. stücke	=	2	=	0	0	3
1 Vier und zwanzig-tha., *or* 1 grs......	=	1	=	0	0	1½

Scheidemünze. (*Division Money.*)

Silver and Copper.

				£	s.	d.
1 Halbe groschen	=	$\frac{1}{48}$ of a dollar	=	0	0	0¾
1 Ein dreier of silver or copper	=	$\frac{1}{96}$ do.	=	0	0	0⅜

Copper.

		£	s.	d.
1 Vier pfennig stücke	=	0	0	0½
1 Ein dreier	=	0	0	0⅜
2 Pfennig (12 *of which* = 1 *groschen*)	=	0	0	0⅓

Observe.—In the course of exchange the *Louis d'or* is generally meant ; the nominal value of which is 5 *dollars*, but it equals 5 *dols.* 12 *gros.* convention money. There are no dollars coined in *convention money*, but there are government *notes*, which represent 1 dol. and 2 dols. *convention money.* There are also 1 and 2 dollar notes, on blue paper, representing Prussian money : these readily pass at their nominal value, an office being established where they may be exchanged for silver. In Saxony, paper money is not a legal tender.

The *Species thaler*, *gulden*, and *half gulden*, or *florin*, are now merely used in trade, and fluctuate in value according to the demand.

FRANKFORT, BADEN, NÜRENBERG, &c. reckon in *Gulden* or *florins* at 60 *kreutzers* each *Rhenish.*

Gold Coins.

		Convention, or 20 gulden fuss			Rhenish, or 24 gulden fuss					
		Guild	*krs.*		*Guild*	*krs.*		£	s.	d.
1 Friedrichs d'or, August d'or, Carl d'or, *or* 5 thaler piece ..	=	7	30	=	9	0	=	0	15	0
1 Ducat, *or* ducaten	=	4	18	=	5	10	=	0	8	7

Silver Coins.

		Convention,			Rhenish,					
		gul.	*kr.*		*gul.*	*kr.*		£	s.	d.
1 Species-thaler (*Conv.*)	=	2	0	=	2	24	=	0	4	0
1 Prussian *or* rix dollar.........	=	1	37	=	1	44	=	0	3	0
1 Halbspecies dollar, *or* gulden	=	1	0	=	1	12	=	0	2	0
1 Halb gulden, *or* ½ florin....	=	0	30	=	0	36	=	0	1	0

GERMAN MONEYS.

SILVER AND COPPER MIXED.

1 Kopfstücke, or 20 kr. Stücke	=	0 20	= 0 24	=	0 0	8
1 Halb do. or 10 kr. stücke..	=	0 10	= 0 12	=	0 0	4
1 Viertel do. or fünf kr. stücke	=	0 5	= 0 6	=	0 0	2
1 Sechs kreutz. stücke. or piece	=	0 5	= 0 6	=	0 0	2
1 Batzen.....................	=	0 3⅔	= 0 4	=	0 0	1⅓
1 Drei kreutz. stücke, or piece	=	0 2½	= 0 3	=	0 0	1

COPPER COINS.

1 Kreutzer stücke, or piece.............	= 0	1	=	0 0	0½
1 Pfennig (obs. 4 pfn. = 1 kreutzer)	= 0	0¼	=	0 0	0¹⁄₁₂

Observe.—The *Prussian dollar* generally passes in *Frankfort* for 1 gulden 44 *to* 45 kreutzers, *Rhenish money.*

MECKLENBURG, ROSTOCK, and WEIMAR, reckon in *dollars* at 1⅓ new ⅔ stücke, or *piece*, each *zwei drittel stücke* being = 32 schillinge = about 2s. 3d. sterling. 1 *Mark Cöln*, which = 40 shilling sterling = nearly 18 new ⅔ pieces.

HANOVER.

Here they formerly used, as the *circulating medium, Cassengeld*[1] but now they adopt the 21 gulden fuss, or *Prussian standard*, called also *Graumannsche Fuss*. They reckon the dollar at 24 gute groschen, or 36 marien groschen, and each *gute groschen* at 12 pfennige.

REAL COINS IN GOLD.

	Thaler. g. Gr.		£ s. d.
1 George d'or, or Louis d'or	= 5	10 convention money	= 0 16 8
1 Ducaten, or ducat	3 0	do.	= 0 9 3

* *Observe.*—*Cassengeld* (literally *broken money*) means the *circulating medium.*

SILVER COINS.

These are nearly the same as the *Prussian coins,* but instead of *Silver groschen,* they have *Marien groschen.*

		Gute gros.	Mar. gros.	£ s. d.
1 Thaler, *or* rix dollar, Prussian standard	=	24	= 36	= 0 3 1½
1 Zwei-drittel stücke, *or* reichs gulden..	=	16	= 24	= 0 2 3
1 Drittel stücke, *or* halbe gulden	=	8	= 12	= 0 1 0½
1 Sechstel stücke	=	4	= 6	= 0 0 6¼
1 Achtel Pfennig	=	2	= 3	= 0 0 3⅛

GERMAN MONEYS.

SCHEIDEMÜNZE, COPPER AND SILVER.

	Pfennige.		£	s.	d.
1 Zwei marien groschen stücke...... =	16	cassengeld =	0	0	2
1 Gute groschen = 1½ marien groschen .... =	12	do. =	0	0	1½
1 Marien groschen stücke......... =	8	do. =	0	0	1
1 Mattier, *or* Matthier .... =	4	do. =	0	0	0½

COPPER COINS.

	£	s.	d.
1 Drei pfennig-stücke .... =	0	0	0⅜
1 Zwei pfennig-stücke .... =	0	0	0¼
1 Ein und halb pfennig stücke .... =	0	0	0$\frac{3}{16}$
1 Pfennig... =	0	0	0⅛

Exchange with London 6 thalers 13 groschen, more *or* less, according to the course of exchange = one pound sterling.

GERMAN WEIGHTS.

AVOIRDUPOIS WEIGHT.

Berlin	100 lbs.	= 114·7	lbs. Eng.	= 107·37 lbs.	Hamburgh
Danzic	do.	= 103·12	do.	= 96·54	do.
Frankfort ..	do.	= 111·41	do.	= 104·30	do.
Hamburg ..	do.	= 106·8	do.	= 100·00	do.
Hanover....	do.	= 107·94	do.	= 101·05	do.
Königsburg	do.	= 103·12	do.	= 96·64	do.
Leipsic	do.	= 103·00	do.	= 96·42	do.
Or 1 Center =	110 lbs=	113·30	do.	= 106·07	do.
Vienna....	100 lbs=	123·48	do.	= 115·60	do.

Observe.—1 Cöln Mark = 3608 grains English, which = 7 oz. 10 dwts. 8 grains English Troy Weight.
Therefore 100 Marks = 751½ English ounces.
100 Marks at Frankfort = 752.2 oz. English Troy Weight.

MEASURES.

LONG MEASURE.

Bavaria	100 ells	= 91·10	yards English.
	100 feet	= 95·75	feet	do.
	1 foot	= 11·49	inches	do.
Berlin	100 ells	= 72·94	yards	do.
	100 feet	=102·97	feet	do.
	1 foot	= 12·35	inches	do.

GERMAN MEASURES.

Frankfort-*on-the-*	100 ells	= 59·95 yards	English
Maine	100 feet	= 93·35 feet	do.
	1 foot	= 11·20 inches	do.
Hamburgh	100 ells	= 62·64 yards	do.
	100 feet	= 94·00 feet	do.
	1 foot	= 11·28 inches	do.
Hanover	100 ells	= 63·86 yards	do.
	100 feet	= 95·80 feet	do.
	1 foot	= 11·49 inches	do.
Leipsic................	100 ells	= 61·71 yards	do.
	100 feet	= 92·69 feet	do.
	1 foot	= 11·12 inches	do.

Observe.—The *Rheinland,* or *Prussian foot,* is equal to 12·35 English inches, the same as for *Berlin, Cologne,* &c., and therefore 1 English foot = 0·9710373 Cologne foot.

The *German,* or *geographical mile,* (15 of which make a *degree* on the equator and equal 69½ English miles nearly) = 4.63 *miles,* or 8150 English yards nearly.

The *Prussian* or *long mile,* of which 14¾ make a degree = 4·7 *miles English.*

MEASURES OF CAPACITY.
CORN MEASURE.

Bavaria (*Baiern*)	100 metzen	= 12·745 Eng. imp. qrs.	
Berlin	100 scheffel	= 18·9	do.
Bremen.............. 1 last=	40 scheffel	= 10·19	do.
Brunswick.............	100 hunter	= 10·72	do.
Danzic and Königsberg	10 lasts	= 106·75	do.
Frankfort a. M.	100 malter	= 39·46	do.
Hamburgh .... 1 last =	30 scheffel	= 10·863	do.

Observe.—In *wheat, rye, beans,* and peas at Hamburgh, 1 scheffel = 2 fasz = 2·8968 English bushels ; and 1 last = 30 scheffel = 3 wispel = 10·863 quarters English ; but in *barley* and *oats* 1 scheffel = 3 fasz ; and 1 last = 20 scheffel, *or* 2 wispel.

At Stettin and Anclam....... 1 last = 13⅞ to 14⅛ Imp. quarters.
— Stralsund and Wolgast .. 1 last = 13⅞ to 14⅛ do.
At the latter places *oats* are an exception.

LIQUID MEASURES.

30 Hamburg viertel	= 47·8 English imperial gallons.	
125·85 Stübschen in Hamburgh....	= 100 gals. Eng. wine measure.	
154·95 ....do............	= 100 do. beer measure.	
At Cöln 1 Ahm..................	= 30·42 English imperial gallons.	
Bavaria 1 Schenk-eimer	= 14·12	do.
Berlin 1 Eimer wein.	= 15·12	do.
1 Tonne bier	= 25·2	do.
Frankfort a. M. 1 Ohm = 20 viertel= 31·569		do.

Printed by Wertheimer, Lea & Co., Circus Place, Finsbury.

www.ingramcontent.com/pod-product-compliance
Lightning Source LLC
Chambersburg PA
CBHW020822230426
43666CB00007B/1063